D1193543

Views of You In Shaded Hues

A Place Between Black and White

Author of *The Up Side of Down*

Alice Nixon-Barr

authorHOUSE®

AuthorHouse™
1663 Liberty Drive, Suite 200
Bloomington, IN 47403
www.authorhouse.com
Phone: 1-800-839-8640

First published by AuthorHouse   10/8/2008

ISBN: 978-1-4343-9751-5 (sc)

Library of Congress Control Number: 2008907982

Printed in the United States of America
Bloomington, Indiana

This book is printed on acid-free paper.

Biblical References: KJV Holy Bible

Materials from 1998-2008

Assistant Editors: Jetta K. Brickell & Angelina Barr

The presenting of an individual's work or the mentioning of their name in this book, in no way constitutes their endorsement of its contents.

Selection from "The Up Side Of Down"
Published May 2006 by AuthorHouse

The Up Side Of Down: The Introduction of A Writer Named Alice
Publisher: AuthorHouse 2006
ISBN: 1-4259-2763-7(e)
ISBN: 1-4259-2762-9 (sc)

CONTENTS

ACKNOWLEDGMENTS

My being alive is because of God; therefore I thank him for giving me a hearing ear, discerning spirit, "Seeing Eye" and compassionate heart. I thank him for the trials that have strengthened me, tragedies that have formed my opinions and common sense that gives me insight.

I thank my children (Sonya Nixon, April Barr (deceased), Samuel Barr, III, Angelina Barr, Helena (Barr) Gray, Deon Barr and James Gray), my son-in-law Stephen Kane and my grandchildren (Jetta Brickell, James Gray, Jr., Ferdinand Salva, Jr., Tiffany Gray and Ashley Gray) for their love and for permitting me to share their lives.

To my brother Grant Williams, Jr., now deceased, again I say thank you for all that you have done for me. I also acknowledge my other siblings, Richard Lee Jones (deceased) and Lelia Savannah Nixon.

I send love to Mrs. Venus Catoe, my friend of 27 years. I thank God for Venus, her husband Raymond and his mother, Mrs. Mabel R. Catoe (deceased).

Thank you Susan Ross of Roslyn, New York for introducing me to Dorine O'Garro, author of "Montserrat On My Mind" and "Montserrat In The Heart." Ms. O'Garro pointed me to a publishing company, as Verneda C. White; author of "God's Ever Watching Eyes" had done for her. Later Ms. O'Garro referred me to her Pastor, Reverend Joy Clarke of St. Peter's Lutheran Church in Springfield Gardens, New York, where

I brought their 2006 Women's Day message. I found Pastor Clarke to be a most dynamic and progressive shepherd.

I congratulate Hazelin Williams of Uniondale, New York, who authored "Too Far North is South" and "Words to Reconstruct You." I also mention Maxwell C. Wheat, Jr. of Freeport, New York, who authored "Iraq and Other Killing Fields, Poetry for Peace."

Special thanks of support to Izora Robinson, Jacob Robinson (deceased), Gloria Gregory and Cherryanne Weinstein. Also Neritza Vera, Brittany, Carmen Rosa and my Texas Rose, Mary Jo Grier. Beverly Rasher and Jerry Dorph of North Carolina, I love you guys. Thank you Roosevelt and Uniondale Public Libraries of Long Island, New York, for making my first book (The Up Side Of Down, The Introduction of a Writer Named Alice) available to the public. Also a special thanks to my aunt Mattie Hoffman and Dr. Burke Cunha, of W.U.H., for their support.

I thank my children and grandchildren for their full support of my works, which represents me. I love you all and am proud of you. Through my works, you will hear my voice of guidance when I have been taken up someday by God.

Finally, to writers and support personnel who refuse to share information or assistance to other aspiring writers, I say, that there is room for all of us. If you keep your hands closed, nothing will go out but nothing can come in either. The same apply to those who can provide start up business assistance to writers including magazine companies, bookstores and places that offer literature for sale. Remember that self-published authors not only write books but they purchase your merchandise. I encourage you to acknowledge their works. Additionally, I encourage organizations and businesses to utilize the services of your community poets and writers. Their works may not always be flawless but it often tells it like it T-I-S. Also remember that every known author was once unknown to you and the world.

FOREWORD

Although I walk through the valley of the shadows of death daily, I refuse to allow fear to overtake me. You see, if I allow fear in, it will mess me up. It will prevent me from obeying the commands of God and cause me to lose my blessings.

Then what do you do when the task before you cause fear to grip your heart? When you know beyond a doubt that it is God who has called you to the place that you must enter, what do you do? Do you go ahead when everything inside of you says DANGER, DANGER or do you run away in an attempt to save your flesh?

While freedom is a human right, even in 2008 some people are guilty of limiting the freedom of others. Many do this out of misplaced fear and others are afraid of losing control.

Fear is a powerful tool of destruction, and if housed in the wrong minds, can cause the destruction of individuals, countries and the world. An example of this is seen through the death of former Prime Minister, Benazir Bhutto an opposition leader in Pakistan. It did not matter that this was a woman, mother and grandmother. I say to you, don't allow fear in for it will mess you up.

Then we see a worse enemy in people who do to others what they claim to hate. Light skin clans thinking themselves better than their darker skin relatives and darker skin relatives hating them for it. Many excuse their behavior by blaming slavery. Others attempt to make a distinction between themselves and others, by pointing to their place of birth and language spoken.

It is ironic since most people in their twenties and thirties have never experienced true slavery. Most have not even experienced the segregation of the South. Their hatred is often based on what the old guard has taught them.

Sadly, neither side seems to remember that we came from and many sucked at the breast of dark skinned mothers, in-spite of who fathered them. Many seem to forget, that at the end of the day, it matters not what part of the world you came from, what language you speak, how much money you have or the hues of your skin, for it is said, that one drop of Black blood makes you Black; not one drop of White blood makes you White.

Whatever our mixtures, we were created in God's image. How then can any of us hate what God so loves and how can any of us despise and not call excellent what he has done? How can any of us hate anyone's skin color when we did not choose it? That includes our own. If we want to despise something, let it be the actions that are committed by others in arrogance and ignorance.

I ask each of you to remember that you did not determine your skin color or the parents you were born to. Further, to deny any part of your heritage is to say that you are ashamed of the love your ancestors had for one-another and you despise God's work.

Furthermore, in case you have not noticed, while many attempt to separate themselves by skin color, an increasing number of people are falling in love with and marrying people across color lines. Also noteworthy is the number of people who are learning of their mixed heritage.

Let us look on the character of one-another and keep skin color out of it. After all, that would be one thing less to trash others over.

Together, African, Asian, Black, Caucasian, Indian, Latina, etc., we are strong; as with the 300 Spartans whose strength was not in their numbers but their unity. They stood together; held ground together and ultimately caused Sparta to win through their willingness to die together. There was no separating or saving of oneself. While each wore frontal armor, their backs were covered by each other. What about you? Today is your chance to make a difference.

Who would have believed that in 2008, any Southern State would have voted in the manner that Alabama, Georgia, Mississippi, South Carolina and Virginia did for a Multinational/Black person? Look at Idaho, Alaska, Minnesota, Connecticut, the District of Columbia, Hawaii and Maryland. Even in states Senator Barack Obama did not win like Indiana, look at the number of votes this man received. I applaud every individual and individual State for your growth and courage.

I suggest that we all come together and stop being out to get each other. Together we can make this nation strong if we stop trying to establish ourselves as better than another. We are of the human race; a species that are "alleged" to be of a higher order than other genus. I believe that it is time that we act like it.

Other nations are watching us. Also remember that the United States of America is multinational. Then why cannot we come together as one?

Maybe you never learned this, but LOVE is what covers our various faults and not hate or indifference. Just like this nation came together for the victims of 911 and other disasters, why can't we remain together in good times?

We have a chance again to heal and recover from our state of decline and denial. Together the people can bring about change. After all, we are better together than separate.

Let us create better tomorrows that generational curses may be broken. Do it for our children and country. Why, because we are a great people and nation.

The jury is yet out on us. We have time to balance the scales of justice. Remember this too, that not only are other nations looking to us, but God is watching us.

SPECIAL DEDICATIONS

MY MOTHER'S INFLUENCE

I learned how to kneel and pray to my father God.
> *not to grovel with God but to ask for what I think I need.*
> *how to weather the storms of life.*
> *to be thankful for what I have and more will come.*
> *to acknowledge the winds of change.*
> *holy boldness. No more would of, could of or should of, because life is too short.*

I learned that without trust you have nothing.
> *I should not second guess myself. My first thought is what flows from within.*
> *to have faith in myself; feel as if the thing is here.*
> *you teach others how to treat you.*
> *to be silent and still when I don't know what to do.*
> *failure is experiences that we are supposed to go through not vacation in.*
> *you never stop learning.*

I learned that life is bigger than me.
> *I am a direct reflection of my family.*
> *family is important.*
> *generational curses can be broken.*
> *not to take things personal when family and people hurt you because they will disappoint you.*

I learned to pay my debt.
> *to shop for bargains.*
> *to be sensible and never pay more than something is worth.*

I learned that a mother's love is priceless.

> *sometimes a mother is all her children have so a true mother will protect them.*
> *a good mother's job doesn't stop when the child is 18.*
> *you will hear your mother's voice when talking to your children.*

I learned how to kick males to the curve.

> *there is a difference between a man and a male.*
> *it's nice to have a man but you don't need one.*
> *never let a man borrow money without a signed receipt.*
> *a real man knows the care of children come first and won't feel the need to compete with them.*
> *a real man builds his house, not lay on a woman's back.*

My mother's influence is like a warm hand giving me guidance, wisdom, love, hope, protection and peace. That is why on this Mother's Day when I find myself financially challenged, I remembered that my words hold more value than any dollar ever could.

Angelina Z. Barr, Happy Mother's Day 2006 to my Mom

I APOLOGIZE

Last night while sitting in my bed thoughts of you went through my mind. I was thinking of how you give me gifts beyond that I expect or want to accept. I listened at myself instructing you all not to purchase me anything over $10.00, and that in 2006. As I explained, having God and each other was all that I needed.

When we were discarded like trash from our home and separated by the man who said I do, God was the only one who watched over us. You see babies; momma can do without a lot, as long as I know that you all are all right.

Unconsciously I had caused you pain. It took God to open my eyes and then allow me to feel how you felt when I instructed you about giving to me. I said don't because you have children to support. In my effort to care for you, I had failed to remember that "It is more blessed to give than to receive." Acts 20:35 KJV

Then I asked myself, why do you think that it is all right to bless them and not realize that God can place it upon their hearts to bless you? Also, why have you failed to see that your words are cutting off their blessings, if they fail to obey God?

All I could say to God was, "I APOLOGIZE." Now I say to each of you, "I APOLOGIZE." I apologize for not seeing that the same God, who moved me to act, also moved you to give. "I APOLOGIZE" for almost cutting your blessings off. "I APOLOGIZE" for pulling back when you pressed on and gave me in-spite of my insisting that you not. "I APOLOGIZE" for being over zealous in my motherly duties, for when God move you to act, do it! Otherwise I say that your prayers and love is enough for this mother.

Also remember that all is acceptable by God according to what you would do if you could. I accept phone calls, hand written notes, text messages, prayers and e-mails.

Now I give you your props for sticking to what I have taught you and what you have seen me do. This is one time that disobeying me was necessary that you too may be blessed.

Thank you for giving me flowers while I can smell them and flowery words while I can hear them. Thank you for your love and accepting my instructions.

In that day when our bodies cease to function and our spirits take flight, know that there will be no reason for any of us to say, "I APOLOGIZE." When all is said and done and friends who were acquaintances are gone, God, Jesus and family will remain.

I love you my children and keep breathing for you. I love all who have called me mother and have made me smile. Most of all, as I have taught you to do, "I APOLOGIZE."

BACK TO BACK FOR OUR CHILDREN'S SAKE

Alone I am weak. Alone I will fail, except for God who has placed me back to back. Back to back I, no back to back we. He has placed me back to back with thee.

Forced we were like lava from a volcano to rise to the top. It was never our intention to lead but we sought to follow. Time and time again we were faced with the decision to go that our children not lose out. Back-to-back, time and time again he became she and she became we.

Back to back you and I kept rising to the occasion. Forced by the integrity that we have learned from our parents and that in turn we cannot separate ourselves. Why? Our heartstrings are tied to our children, our community and our pride. Why? Because deep down inside, the red blood that keep pumping within us, pushes us on to win the race by faith. Endurance is the key it says.

He positioned us and not of our choice. He has called us and we cannot hide. We were like two warriors waiting for orders from a ghost captain. Being left to fend for ourselves, we decided to climb out of the three feet wide darkened hole. Separate we could do nothing, but together and back-to-back we climbed to challenges that our children may live.

We are but ordinary women that God called to an extraordinary task. He gave us strength of character and an ear to hear. God provided us with examples in Mother Warriors, whose hearts have taught us how to turn back to back that we may come forward in power.

Dedicated To: Ms. Angelina Barr, Mrs. Rhonda Cherry and Mrs. Maureen Powell of Roosevelt, Long Island, New York.

LIFE IN A CIRCLE I CAME FACE TO FACE WITH MY BEGINNING

Everything has a beginning and even an end, but what is done in the middle I will meet face to face in the end.

Before a here, now, when, who or where you were there. I had no consciousness of this world; a mother or father, yet you knew me. Brought to be in a day and time not of my choosing and formed in a womb from a thought, act, egg and sperm was I.

You created me and not by accident but design. It was you that loved me first and have given me those who cherish me. You have kept me through the highs, lows and continue to keep me grounded.

God you are the one that has made life worth living. You provided sunshine even when tears fell as rain from Heaven. It is you that have kept me close to your heart; fully human and fully alive. You were the one who chose my love, my life and husband Gregory.

Even as I find myself in this hard place, I know that I am not alone. Through Jesus and you I am alive another two years.

Life in a circle is all that it is and I have come face to face with my beginning that I may know, that my ending is in your hands. Without fear or worry this I do know that my ending shall be better than my beginning.

Dedicated to Mrs. Kathryn Pisani and
The Spirit of Those Surviving Major Illnesses

YOU TWISTED MY WORLD

In one moment and with premeditation, you made a decision that twisted my world. Without caring of the impact to me, your family, mine or even yourself, you took my innocence, my faith in humanity and men. Instead of looking out for me, you and your boy(s) held me down and with brutality defiled me.

Because of you my world is twisted. My ability to trust, date and marry is now in question. You, yes you my brothers, you became my rapist and then went on to kick me as if I had done something wrong. While I was helpless, not one of you came to my rescue. You are twisted males that devalue women.

Hear this ye males, what you did to me on yesterday, you will pay for. Not by me or mine, but vengeance is God's. Romans 12:19 KJV says, "Dearly beloved, avenge not yourselves, but rather give place unto wrath: for it is written, vengeance is mine; I will repay, saith the Lord."

You should never have touched God's anointed. While you saw only me, you failed to see the angels watching and keeping you from killing me. You, yes you were not your sister's keeper but the worst type of abuser.

Instead of protecting me my brothers, you have caused my world to be twisted. My dreams, aspirations and desire to stay close to any man have all been twisted because of you, you and you.

Because of you this Mother's Day for my mother was filled with sadness and my father wept. My grandmother said "Stay your hands, because God will avenge her." You, yes you my so called brothers twisted my world. You held me down and one by one raped me as God looked down and cried. The tears were not for me, but you and yours.

In time he will heal me and help me overcome what you have done, but your actions will throughout History put a stain on your families.

Didn't your mothers teach you to love and respect young ladies and women? Didn't they tell you that your sins will be visited upon your children; your daughters and even them? Well if you did not know, I am here to tell you, "Be not deceived; God is not mocked; for whatsoever a man soweth, that shall he also reap." Galatians 6:7 KJV.

I lay there wounded in the house of what I thought was a friend. Now I understand what my mother and grandmother meant when they said, "Friends won't hurt you but will protect you." "Friends are few and if you have one in a lifetime you are blessed." Everyday Nanny says, "Baby watch as well as pray." Now I understand why they said "God and family" is all I can count on.

Although I suffered and have much to endure, if it stop you from hurting someone else it won't be in vain. Now I pray to God that my body is not infected with AIDS or a commutable disease. Yes I paid a high price for this life lesson, but yours will be higher.

Yes you twisted my world, but God in his goodness will make it right someday. As I grown older and possibly marry a man that is not of my race, please don't ask me why. It will be because when I look at them, I don't see your face(s).

Dedicated to the Survivors of Rape

JUST FOR ME

You did it all and just for me. You suffered unmentionable acts, ate what dogs wouldn't, held your friends as they drew their last breath and even watched them die. You, yes I am talking to every Veteran from World War I to the Iraq War. Young, old, here or gone, you did it all for me. You who dared go, bled and even died all just for me. You who sacrificed your limbs, family life, eyesight and health just for me. In-spite of the hardships and instead of running away, you stood there and did it all just for me.

You took the abuse, acceptance, denials, rejections and even disrespect all just for me. You, yes you and even you that died, you all are my heroes.

Done not just for glory but to protect those you held and continue to hold dear. You never inquired of my worthiness or the country that you served, but you just took up arms and did it all for me.

With humility and the kiss of love, I thank you from World War I, World War II, the Korean War, Vietnam War, Afghanistan, Desert Storm, Gulf conflict, Iraq War and any I failed to name. Thank you for helping God keep me alive for one more day.

Presented April 2007
To Army 1st Lieutenant Gene J. Takahashi
Who passed shortly after receiving this presentation.
Also
To all Military Personnel

VIEWS OF YOU IN
SHADED HUES

Peering through the branches on trees in the forest, I saw only a portion of the sky. From where I stood, I could only see clear blue skies, but out of view dark clouds were rising.

Often what we cannot see is what becomes the problem. Without my knowing, a portion of the blue sky had turned dark, torrential rains began to fall, thunder rolled and lightning flashed. I turned to run for cover only to see on the horizon a cone shaped cloud whirling and churning my way. With torrential rains falling on me and a tornado whirling before me, I found myself trapped. If I had listened to the weather announcements or took time to view the skies around me, I would not have been trapped.

Too often in life people are so busy working for things and enjoying pleasures that they lose focus on what really matters. While they busy themselves trying to amass wealth, fighting for positions, scraps and destroying one-another, the enemy has laid traps that will take away everything they own. Often their children walk around as if oblivious to the real world. They think there are no repercussions for their actions, and they have been snared by the trappings of society. They are attracted by flashy jewels, cars and clothing that many parents give them to replace love and attention. Usually this type gets into all kinds of trouble and disregard laws that were meant to maintain order. They do this thinking their parents' money can get them out of anything. Their confidence is in things and money, not God and morality.

Then you have those that desire what others have. Many watch the rich and want to be accepted in their circles. Some attempt to prove that they can have the same things their peers have and will attempt to acquire them by any means. They have been trapped by societal greed. Often their seeking to gain things is at the expense of their family values, their freedom and sometimes their lives. Unfortunately, their self-worth is tied to possessions and not character.

People that attract them often are the wrong type of company. Then family members are left to hire psychiatrist, doctors, lawyers and plead before judges for help for their children. They beg our government to pass just laws and to provide additional funding to educate our children instead of funding more prisons.

Don't parents and children know that there is big money in dysfunction? Don't they know that prisons are a big business and that depending on your clan, you can be put away for life or have your life altered forever?

They don't get that there is no such thing as a "free lunch." Everything costs something of somebody! Your time, money, character and life or that of others. Your value as a human being, freedom and your future.

While many that are rich sit in their little world believing they are invincible, and insulated by their money from the rest of the world, they have deceived themselves. The truth is that even water will eventually seep into what is termed waterproof. When they become comfortable in their way of living, the outside world enters and turns their neat world upside down.

Oppression can lead to bloodshed and lost of life. "Live and let live" is crucial to all our survival as is being our "brothers and sisters keepers."

Even many who have tasted a lifestyle that they cannot afford will do just about anything to continue that lifestyle. They have foolishly taken their rent money, lunch money, diaper or light bill money to purchase a Coach cell phone holder for over $100., a pair of Air Jordan sneakers for over $100. or some celebrities perfume that they cannot afford. Then they get angry and steal from others in an attempt to satisfy a false feeling of entitlement. We read about them in newspapers, watch them on crime shows and hear about them on radios.

Then you have the middle class who are busy trying to obtain the "American dream," amass wealth like the rich or simply maintain a reasonable style of living. Many work long hours, make purchases beyond their means and get their children accustomed to a lifestyle they cannot afford. They wear expensive clothing, shoes and jewelry. They attend private schools with the rich and famous, but are skating on fumes. Their cars say rich as does their homes, but they are in debt pass their necks.

With credit card debt mounting faster than the cost of living wage increases, they are heading for a fall. Worse than that, their children have become accustomed to a lifestyle they cannot afford. Instead of facing reality and coming clean, often parents hide from friends and family who they really are. It causes me to wonder if they have considered the effect that their poor lifestyle choices will have on their children when they become adults.

Will their children connect with the unscrupulous or turn to crime in an attempt to maintain a lifestyle they cannot afford?

Will they grow up and follow their parent's footsteps or will they have the courage to live within their means? Will they understand the difference between having things and things having control over them?

These are they who are struggling to simply keep their heads above water and provide their basic needs. These are the middle class that are becoming the poor class.

What about the poor, often referred to as the forgotten? Many work hard and cannot get a leg up on expenses. The more they try the deeper in debt they get. They are one pay check from being homeless and having to go on public assistance. Often this lead to anger which can turn to envy and jealousy, which often leads to criminal behavior.

Some even resort to committing unthinkable acts in an attempt to gain things. Then we wonder why prisons are full of the poor and working poor-middle class. After all it is the middle class who funds the poor class and pay where the rich get big tax breaks. Where is the economic balance for all?

While we worry about material things, we have failed to keep our eyes on those in leadership positions. Many are gathering to themselves our hard earned money and spending it as they please. Our money is funding a war that we should never have been involved in. Make no mistake; the billions of dollars being sent to Iraq are not all staying in Iraq. This we would know if we had not relinquished our authority to those not deserving of our trust.

We the people of the United States of America have left "the fox in charge of the hen house," and we have failed to learn from past mistakes. Without protest, most Americans embrace cabinet members who are themselves "wolves dressed in sheep's clothing."

The people grin from ear to ear when they are in their presence, as if they are movie stars. Most fail to remember that movie stars are actors and actresses that are hired to give great performances. Who they really are does not matter if they can perform, and their name recognition bring in crowds to produce millions of dollars. When the lights of Broadway go down and the performance is over, what are we left with? What condition have these elected officials left our country in for our children and ourselves? Then you wonder why I have "Views of You In Shaded Hues."

Diversion tactics keep us busy watching increasing oil prices, escalating taxes, utility surcharges and trying to hold on to jobs that fail to keep up with the cost of living. On the back side we are hemorrhaging. For every dollar given to us, thousands more are taken. We are being drowned in our own vomit and the ones holding our heads down won't even turn them sideways to keep us from dying.

We can no longer pray aloud in schools and questions have been raised about courtrooms displaying, "In God We Trust" signs. Some question others loyalty if they don't display the American flag on their lapel.

Wearing a flag doesn't make one patriotic. Neither does, saying America's own actions will cause her damnation make one unpatriotic.

Lawmakers who are lawbreakers made it where Mothers and fathers can no longer chastise their children with spankings when necessary and I did not say beatings, but the police can kill them.

Our leadership is at the bottom of our struggles and our allowing ourselves to be turned away from godly principles.

We pay so much in taxes that we pay taxes on taxes. What do we get in return? Foreclosed homes, loss of jobs, incompetent leaders and from all walks of life. I ask you, are you yet wondering why I have "Views of You in Shaded Hues?"

My daughter Zoë saw a bumper sticker that said, "When Bill Clinton lied nobody died." I add to that, "When George Bush lied thousands died" and more are yet dying.

Our failure to at least investigate information given us is mostly due to our being lazy. We have given too much authority to those not worthy of our trust. The damage done could have been minimal if we had paid closer attention to those making decisions on our behalf. Now we are faced with financial ruin and our nation's moral decline.

Past indiscretions can be forgiven since none of us are perfect. Also childish youth is one thing, but continued bad behavior by adults is another. Further, why are the people being held to a higher standard than lawmakers and those in pulpits?

Too many blind have led the blind and too many wolves are garbed in sheep's clothing. It is time to take control of our lives and our country that we may live. It's time to kneel down in prayer that we may emerge victorious. The word of God tells us that, "If my people which are called by my name will humble themselves, pray, seek my face and turn from their wicked ways, then will I hear from Heaven and will forgive their sins and heal their land." The USA is morally sick and almost spiritually bankrupt.

What America teach other nations against, they allow and do themselves. Other nations are not in denial, as many in America are. They have and continue to see what the hypocrisy *of many here has done to the disenfranchised in this country, and see the damage that is being done in other countries. Many would rather die than allow their country to be taken over by America.*

Other nations see this and despise America's leadership for it. They wonder why the American people don't rise against corrupt leaders in their own country and demand their removal from office, as our nation's leaders have done in foreign countries. Thou hypocrites, how can you attempt to take the moth out of their eyes and not remove the beam from your own? How can Hillary Clinton who is Caucasian, title a book using one of our oldest and most treasured African/Black American proverbs; "It Takes a Village to Raise a Child," without our permission, then accuse Senator Barack Obama of plagiarism when he used words from his friend, Gov Deval Patrick of Massachusetts? Did we say of her, just like Columbus said he discovered America; I guess she discovered our proverb? No, that is childish, because we all quote others from time to time.

Furthermore, did Senator Obama accuse her of plagiarism, when she kept quoting his words of "Yes, We Can" and "Fired Up, Ready to Go?" Why is it all right for her to do that but not Senator Obama? Double standards again. Yet many are in denial.

I say to the American people, don't let "BBC World News America," be the ones to reveal the lies being told to us. We need to seek the truth ourselves and stop giving trust where not warranted. Never again leave your children, yourselves and your country in the hands of anyone without laying markers of accountability. Open your spiritual eyes that you may see the truth. Open your spiritual ears that you may hear truth and open your mouth and reveal the hidden iniquities of those around you. Know that there is a place between "Black and White." It is called "Shaded Hues."

Yes it is time for change. It is time to give the young ones a chance to do what the old guard did not.

On February 22, 2008, the night before my 57th birthday, I watched BET HONORS. Tyra Banks told of how she had called her mama from Paris some years ago to tell her that she "couldn't do it anymore." Her mother did not take over, but she quit her job here in America and went to Paris to be strength for her daughter. In public and without any reason to be ashamed, Tyra began to cry as she remembered the love and sacrifice of her mother in loving her. Her mother realized that more than her existence was important. She wanted to make sure her child had a future, therefore she did what was necessary to help her.

She was not selfish; using the about me theme, but thought about her child's future. After all, we are on our way out and it should be our job to help the next generation succeed. This is what our older leaders; older guard should be doing. Instead of holding on so tight to positions that the people are being strangled, they should be backing the younger generation; mentoring them by working with them side by side and relinquishing power over to them while they are alive to help guide them. I speak of people like Senators Edward Kennedy, Hillary Clinton and John McCain. I applaud Senator Edward Kennedy for understanding the vision and following through on it on behalf of Senator Barack Obama.

A WHITE HOUSE WITH A
DARKENED VIEW & ROOF

The house may be white but the roof is darkened and the fumes from within have caused the windows to give off shaded views of the real world.

Human frailties and expectations cause black and white to become shades of gray that a place of compromise may be found. Yet human beings fail to understand that their being flawed and limited causes laws to be flawed in scope. This pompous attitude, make it difficult for mankind to pass sentences that allow the shades of gray to be adopted as a viable middle ground, that others may experience the kind of justice that mercy calls for.

The house may be white but its darkened roof and tinted windows work to shut out fairness to "all." Gray allows black and white to meet and mix their hues that black not be too dark to see the light and the day not to bright that it cause blindness. Grayness gives sunset and evening a chance to blend, that we all may clearly see that we have more in common than our differences sometimes allow us to see.

TODAY YESTERDAY
AND TOMORROW

While standing on today, I found myself looking back on yesterday, as I turned to face tomorrow. Suddenly I realized, that our beginning had much to do with yesterday and today, and that our tomorrows would be determined by today's decisions.

Tears streamed down my face. I had been struck by the awesomeness of God. Wonder of wonders, what was spoken almost 2000 years ago, had shown up at doors today. God had shown up at our door. Front and center had called our names. They overtook us at God's command.

Suddenly we were forced to feel the pain of loss, which yielded temporary unity. World War III in the form of the Iraq War came riding on our heels. Unfulfilled dreams and hopes were dashed to the ground, as children, mothers, wives, husbands, fathers, relatives and friends were left behind.

Then he made quiet my spirit, that I may carefully view America's past. Off came my rose colored blinders that I may see clearly. Then slowly he rolled forward the pictures of America's lifetime and oh what a revelation. Savagery was seen over and over again. "We Trust In God" had become a fashion statement to cover men's hypocrisy. Blood was the foundation of this nation. Native Indians, Negro slaves, aborted babies, civil rights supporters, illegal immigrants and select refugee blood. Economic empowerment dripped with the blood of those having faced economic enslavement. Religiosity, discrimination, prejudice and bigotry dripped with the blood of the innocent.

Death by cop, silenced prayers in schools, parents' rights taken and pedophiles loosed in minority communities unfolded. Oh what a condemning revelation of the acts of mankind came forward.

Then I heard blessings and cursing proceeding out of the mouths of those elected to formulate laws for our best interest. Hidden sins were uncovered; that a nation's people may see the evil committed by lawmakers who are themselves lawbreakers.

Justice covered her eyes as the people cried. She that is governed by he could no longer stand to see the twists placed on laws that were formulated by unjust justices. She is not blind, but was incased in justice's ice. Just ice became her name, in that she could not feel any fires of rightness.

Turn, I heard her say. Turn and return to the ways of the creator. Repent, I heard her say. Acknowledge your wrongs that he may forgive you. Forgive, I heard her utter, that you may receive forgiveness. Pull back your hands that he may act on your behalf. For with the forces of nature and his mighty army he fights. His troops are not chosen in great numbers, but by their ability to lap water as they go.

Who can best the Lord? Who can hide from him?

Then over my right shoulder, I saw a sea of blood. It flowed from where two towers once stood; where the streets were rumored to be paved with gold. It was red blood. Red American blood. All races were represented. It had no name, but the color of red.

Then he called for fearless children, ones who would take a stand and speak the truth. He called for ones, which would take off the blinders, acknowledge their sins and repent, that the land may be healed.

With the wave of a hand, God had reached back into our past and pulled up our history. Dirty it was, but clear hearts, clean hands and mountain climbers the red blood made. Then he stood us up straight, that the foolishness of men not cause our demise, and that his story may unfold.

DISORDERS

Be careful of leaches, obsessive people and stalkers; all three are dangerous.

Leaches latch on to others where not invited, in an attempt to suck their life force and finances dry. These types of people believe that what is yours is theirs and that the world owes them a living. Attempt to break free and they may become violent, because they live through you and see you as their means of recognition and survival.

Obsessive people attempt to control your every move, surroundings and associations. Their worth is connected to being aligned with you. You are their possession and personal prize. Any attempt by others to enter what they feel is their space threatens them. Your moving to eliminate them out of your life creates fear and anxiety. If the truth were told, you never included them in your circle, they inserted themselves. Watch out for insurgents and clingy people.

The stalker watches your every move. You have no rights, because they have declared that you are theirs. They are very dangerous and will kill you even if it causes them their freedom or life.

Be very careful of stalkers and those who latch on to you. Often they look just like you and me, but underneath their surface, is a deranged personality.

FALSE POSITIVES

Life is filled with false positives. Faking right while going left, imitating originals and using shameful tactics all are forms of false positives.

I ask, "How can a child bring home A's and B's in Reading, Writing and Arithmetic through Elementary School, then bring D's and F's home through Jr. and Sr. High School?"

Did it ever dawn on you that something is wrong with an individual who is fluent in Spanish in the 9th grade and in the 10th grade cannot speak one sentence of Spanish? I looked at the report card and it said "A." Can you explain what is going on? Either you can read, write and solve math problems or you cannot.

As I sit here and scratch my head, I cannot help but wonder how children who excel from Pre-Kindergarten through the sixth grade, manage to fail grades seven through twelve? How can they graduate high school on par, but cannot complete a job application or write an acceptable college essay?

I do not pretend to have most of the answers, but I believe that lurking in the halls and classrooms of many schools are aberrations of readiness. These false positives are killing our children's dreams, making parents pull their hair out and causing taxpayers to become fed up with tax increases that fail to yield a better education for children.

Then you that cause these failures have the audacity to wonder why I have "Views of You In Shaded Hues."

It is time to get rid of don't care people and systems that rob our children of the rich education they deserve. It is time to weed out those that want to micro-manage school districts in an attempt to elevate themselves and not children. It is time to fire those who are in our schools only to collect paychecks and get the Summer off, while dedicated teachers put in their blood, sweat and tears. It is time to reward excellence and not mediocrity.

The time has come for parents, teachers, students and the community alike, to demand what they pay for and to demand what our children deserve. It is time to reposition ourselves that we may be in the right place, support the right people and keep their feet to the fire.

CONFLICTING BELIEFS

They say that I am out of order because my beliefs conflict with theirs. They say that I need a church home, pastor and church family too. They say that I am disobeying God's commands because I walk outside of their beliefs.

I say that I maintain order by conflicting with their beliefs. I say that I have a church and it is God's that exists in Jesus the Christ. Therefore, I have a pastor and shepherd in the living son of God.

They say that I need a church home; a building that is made with brick, mortar, steel and concrete. It is run by mankind, many that knowingly distort God's word for their profit.

The church Jesus spoke of was built on faith like that of Peter. He preached from the sea, mountains, homes and valleys. If he was and remain our perfect example, why didn't he build large edifices and monuments to leave his name upon? Allow me to answer. It is because souls and the hearts of mankind were his aim not gaining money and fame. That's mankind's game.

They say that no one is perfect, yet they preach and demand my perfection while they live lies. They say how they live is none of my business, but I am commanded by them and their followers, to do what they say, like they say and when they say it.

I say that I am in this state of being after trying it their way so often; wanting to belong so badly and going along to get along. However, I found that I could not swallow or digest their words. They just wouldn't go down, as the spirit in me could not agree with theirs. Now they want to condemn me for not following them while they walk in unrighteousness.

Through the Holy Scriptures, I learned how to distinguish the voice of God from men. However, if I fail to listen to that nudge in my spirit that says, "Take Heed, take heed," I fall into trouble. Why, because being human, I override the radar that God has given me and fall into distress.

It is not always easy to recognize a hireling; wolf in sheep's clothing. We all have to learn to recognize them and God's word has taught us how.

In 1 John 4:1, we were commanded to not believe "every spirit, but try the spirits whether they are of God: because false prophets are gone out into the world."

Too often people try the spirits of people by their spirit instead of by God's word. If your spirit is defective and the person's spirit you are trying your spirit by is defective, you both will fall in the ditch. As apples and oranges cannot grow on the same tree and light and darkness cannot occupy the same space at the same time, nor can good and evil work in agreement.

I believe that you are known by the company you keep. You don't have to say a word, but let me hang around you long enough and I can identify you by the fruit you bear. You can fake it, but not for long. The real person comes through eventually. This is not to say that we have to agree on everything, but there will be an ease of working together because of the spirit of God within.

You see, while you may be able to thrive in mess, I cannot. Further, I refuse to be an enabler or party to lies and filth. I can *work with you and exist in your midst without letting who you are become a part of me.*

If this makes me insubordinate, I wear the badge with honor. Pleasing God is my aim and not following the lost into destruction.

I cannot help light the way for you if I walk in darkness with you, and I cannot agree with you just to get along with you. What I can do is agree with you when you are right, and disagree with you when you are wrong.

I yet need a church home, preacher and family. For what I ask? To bury me, bleed me dry or talk about me?

The dead are to bury the dead and our giving according to how God has blessed us. Instead most churches not only collect offerings and tithes of their members, but command and demand they give unreasonable amounts of money for other ventures.

If we studied the word of God with understanding that comes from God, we would know better and thereby could do better. However, when we obey men before obeying God's word, one day we may look up and find that we were serving mankind and not God. Romans 10:14 KJV

Before you say it, I know that a portion of Romans 10:14 of the KJV says, "How can we hear without a preacher" and that part of the 15th verse says, "How shall they preach, except they be sent?" Part of the problem is that many preaching the word was never called or sent by God to preach. They go on their own or have allowed someone to say they have a calling on their lives to preach. Instead of listening to God, they have a form of godliness but are without any power. Yes, they may be called, but were they sent by God to preach? They may be called but have they allowed God to prepare them? They may be called but for what purpose?

In about 1979 a preacher offered me a "Billy" if I would keep quiet about his love affair and let his girlfriend, who was a member of the church, live with my children and me.

Oh, but that is just one preacher, right oh ye saints? Well in about 1980 another married preacher came to my home before eight AM, fell on his knees and said "God sent me to your house." I told him that God's word said, "Shun the very appearance of evil" and "Don't let your good be evil spoken of." Further, I instructed him to get up off his knees, get in his car and drive back down the one block from my home to his wife's home before my neighbors think that I was having an affair with him.

Not convinced yet that I don't need to be in men's churches? Listen, allow me to set the record straight. You can do what you want to. Just stop telling me that I am going to Hell because I am not a member of a physical building/church. Now back to the subject. In about 1985, a third church pastor had his wife call me to tell me that "I was going to Hell" for giving a needy family the money that God instructed I give them. You see, instead of my putting the tithes in church, I gave the money to this family in East Patchogue, New York.

They were fully aware of my great church hurt. Well, I told her to tell him that I would take my chances with God, since he is the one who told me to do it. Furthermore, I told her to tell her husband that I could not serve under a man that I could not obey. I asked her to thank the church for allowing me to worship with them. Then I said, "If God want to burn me then let him burn me."

I am not finished yet. Well, the last pastor that I sat under in about 1996, told me that he could find me a husband, but if I thought any man was going to be faithful to his wife, I was kidding myself. He knew my history with an abusive and adulterous former spouse. There were witnesses too. Several men and women from the church were sitting around the table in the restaurant with us. I argued the point that a man who has Christ in his life doesn't do such things. He politely laughed and let me know, that "ALL men cheat on their wives." I began to question my being naïve and the possibility that I was raised wrong. I questioned for a moment if I should accept this to have a husband. Then again, I'm not a desperate woman. After all, whatever the economic status, race, color or background, most males believe themselves to be entitled to cheat on their wives. Further, this was my pastor; a man of the cloth; the watchman on the wall for my soul, telling me this. I shook myself and demanded of myself that I not fall for that hogwash. Then I said to myself, "That means he cheats on his wife." I was having none of this mess and said to myself, "Got to go!"

Well, if studying God's word for over "16" years under the auspices of pastors did not teach me to discern the difference between God's shepherds and hirelings, another 25 years sure won't. Besides, I will be held responsible in the end, if I fail to study that God may approve my works as true.

Furthermore, God never said that he would give us only one pastor, but "I will give you pastors according to mine heart, that shall feed you with knowledge and understanding." No man or *woman can be everything to an individual. Digest what you can and leave the rest alone.*

Unfortunately, many in the Black church will crucify you verbally if you say anything against their pastor/their god. They forget that God is God and that the churches keep involving themselves in matters they should not be in anyway. Instead of building the body of Christ, many are the cause of many saints stumbling and falling. Further, no pastor should tell any parishioner how to vote and should be praying for all of the candidates.

Now back to my personal experiences in churches. My black and bruised eyes are down and the man that I was married to since dead. The pastor who told me to put the boxes of nude cards back under the mattress my husband and I slept on, has began a new church. You yet say that I need a church home? Don't you mean that you need me? If for nothing else, you need someone to continue talking about how they walk, act, look and speak.

Helping one another? Money goes in but nothing comes out. Teaching how to entreat one another? Sleeping with my spouse is the flavor of the day.

Tell me, why would I want to subject myself to more of these politically religious, rhetoric spewing hirelings that play at the gospel instead of living it? Why would I sit under someone who leave their people to face a hurricane Katrina or Rita alone and sit themselves up in safety? When will people learn that when the blind lead the blind, they all will fall into the ditch?

Blind pastors leading blind people. Bishop who? Pastor who? Reverend who? Monsieur who? Wake up people and realize that you are following men and women and not God! Wake up before it is too late and get back on the right track! Open your spiritual ears that you can again recognize the voice of God from

31

that of mankind. Take back you place with God and realize that your ability is what will lead you to stability and not the ramblings of fools.

Oh no, come on, don't snatch your wigs off, pull off your high heels and punch me in the eye. I hear you sister saying, "You don't talk about my pastor like that, I will beat you down!" "I will kick your Black ass!" Hold on sister, stop! It is this type of behavior that turns so many people off in church when they come to find peace.

They are greeted with rude, unloving and down right nasty people, who don't want anyone coming in "their church," especially if the new parishioner is gifted.

I'm sorry that you are blind in one eye or both. I'm sorry that you have not seen yet that you are in a church click. I understand, because I was similar to you. Then God asked me a question which opened my eyes. He asked me, "How do you see men?" I answered "what?" Finally he opened up my mind and allowed me to remember the man Jesus had placed mud on eyes and then asked him how do he see men? After washing the mud off his eyes and opening them, he answered, "like trees walking." Jesus asked him again and he answered "as they are." Jesus told him, "then don't go back." Now that my eyes are open, I can no longer act like I don't see what I see or know what I know. What about you? How do you see men?

Do I fall into temptations and make mistakes? Yes! I even knowingly walk into stuff that I should not, but through the consciousness of God within me, I back up and repent.

I lived with you, served with you and am yet acquainted with you. I know that I'm damaged! Can't even you see that I am scarred for life? I know it; God knows it and I hope you too know it.

I am showing my scars; what church folks have done to me and my family, in the hopes that men and women of God will care about their walk with God and in front of others.

You see, I know that I am one of the called of God and chosen by him. I am walking in the vocation to which I was called, what about you?

I can survive you and I do it everyday. What I cannot survive is kicking against the spirit of God.

When I told God that I did not want to write some of the things that I have written in this book, God alerted me, that he didn't need me if I could not do what he commands of me. He told me that you are worried about what men can do to you; kill your body, but you better worry about what I can do to you; "I can destroy your body and soul in Hell's fire."

Just like a loving father, he set me straight. Further he took some of the salt out of my wounds by telling me the reason he chose me.

He said, "I chose you because you have the ability to decrease that I may increase." In other words, I am not a glory hog. Without God I would completely self-destruct. He is the only glue that is capable of holding all of these broken pieces together. He is the one who holds me when I cry at night; being broken hearted and unloved by others. He keeps me in my humanness; my fears and lack. It is he that reminds me, that "perfect love casts out fear."

I hear pastors exclaiming how Bishops are their mentors; seriously flawed Bishops. Flesh and blood looking up to flesh and blood. "Birds of a feather flocking together" and not watching the company that they keep.

Who ordered your steps and who called you? Was it your natural daddy who thinks you should take over the church he pastors or perhaps someone said that God called you to lead? "Pride comes before a fall" people.

Choose God as your mentor and you will never go wrong.

Follow your shepherd as long as they follow God, but don't follow so close that when they error, you cannot see it but follow them into the ditch. Stop depositing your faith into broken vessels and put your faith where it belongs; in God.

Also remember this, that the "GOSPEL" is God's design for our lives.

Allow me to share with you what God showed me about the word "GOSPEL." He broke it down letter by letter for me that I would fully understand his design for my life.

The Gospel is God's plan. He personally designed it that we may obtain everlasting life.

It is

G –"God's
O – own
S – special
P – plan,
E – everlasting
L – life.. (cr)

Further, the letters in BIBLE encapsulates all that we need to make it back to God.

Below I will share the decoding of the letters in BIBLE that I heard by word of mouth and without the author's name being given to me.

> B –"Basic
> I – instructions
> B – before
> L – leaving
> E – Earth."

What an awesome God we serve. He has given us a road map to not only live in this world, but that our actions here will be based on our desire to obtain everlasting life with and not separated from him. Also remember, whom God loves he chasten and if we cannot accept his chastening, he says we are bastards and not his.

Remember that God has a plan for your life. Don't let anyone steal your inheritance and don't attempt to steal theirs.

DEFENDER OR ENEMY

The time has come again for me to question if you are my defender or my enemy? Years ago many of my enemies, wore sheets, hoods and burned crosses on lawns. Many were law enforcement officers and church going people too. Today some that do the same thing are law enforcement officers that wear emblems of justice and peace but are closet racist, murderers and rapist too.

Who do I run to when I'm being threatened and who can my children count on to protect them instead of doing them harm? Are you my defender or my enemy?

Do you see in colors, community lived in or do you take pride in your position? I need you to respond as I look into your eyes. Please answer my question, are you an enemy or friend?

Are you the drug dealer's sponsor or the madam's protection? Are you sniffing more drugs than the crack head on the streets? On your salary, how did you amass such wealth? I see you run stop signs, red lights and commit traffic infractions that are not due to any emergency. If I did this, you would ticket me.

Remember this, when you seek to hang others with the hangman's noose, place a choke hold on a son, draw a gun on a daughter or throw down a weapon, you as fathers and mothers have passed on your sins to your children who follow. This includes lawmakers who are lawbreakers. They use courtrooms to pimp those that error so that their associates from probation officers, lawyers and special services get paid for doing nothing to help those that have broken the law. The bottom line for them is gain and by any means. I wonder what we would find if we looked into their background and that of their family members? I say this to remind you that all families have problems.

One day time and eternity will slap their hands, justice will be received and the just rewarded. Until then, I say, let each of us try to manage the beam in our eye, before attempting to remove the small moth from another's eye.

UP AND DOWN STREAM

Going with the flow is easy, since there is no struggle in swimming down stream, walking down stairs or going along with the decision of others just to get along. Strength and backbone is developed through standing against wrong, climbing steep stairs and fighting strong waves to go upstream.

Believe me when I say, that you will never make it upstream going along with the flow.

He is so smart I hear, yet he is running with criminals. She is so intelligent and beautiful, why is she in a gang?

Didn't they learn anything from going to jail? Smart says, I have learned my lesson and will do better, while slick stick his hand in the lion's mouth again and is consumed.

Even this 2008 election year find the American people fighting strong political waves in an attempt to go upstream.

Don't just go along to get along, but stand up and fight the currents of "doing business as usual," that in the end our children will be the winners.

A PLAUSIBLE STORY

Allow me to tell you a plausible story; one that may have more truth to it than fiction. What if years ago a very brilliant woman planned out her future. She knew that her high aspirations could not be realized at that time. She understood that in order to fulfill her aspirations, she would have to sacrifice who she really was and even her own happiness. She chose a handsome man that could be molded to reach the heights that the times would not allow a woman to reach. She knew what he was and his weaknesses, but she also knew that by helping him become a success, that she could realize her dreams, by piggybacking on his successes that were orchestrated by her. He was outgoing and with ease moved amongst all people.

Slowly the dream began to come to fruition. With her help he achieved great power. The agreement may have been, if I help you amass this power, then you must agree to help me reach my goals too. After all, who is the brain behind this team.

While the amassing of power takes strategic planning, often God with whom there are no entitlements is left out of the equation.

You see, when we least expect, God throws in a David as he did with King Saul. David was described as gangly and the least expected to be called to such a place. Furthermore, David loved King Saul.

Saul had to learn that "Favor isn't fair," as Bishop T. D. Jakes often say. It was God who chose David over King Saul.

Denial and amazement set in. How could this be? Someone who has less experience has not put in the service that I have. There is no way that this is happening to me; not me. This is impossible! This cannot be happening to me, not me! Then King Saul sought to kill David. He and his men hunted for David, but God had David's back. David proved that he could have killed King Saul, but instead he showed him and his family mercy.

2008 nothing new under the sun. Believe what you want to, but out of "the abundance of the heart the mouth speaks," as per God's word. Do you get it?

WHO IS BEHIND YOU

I heard you claim that you authored your successes and future too. It was you who designed yourself, built your image and sustained yourself. Well I am here to say, that if the truth were told, you cannot of yourself do anything. You cannot even draw your next breath without help.

While the world observes you in your power and glory, they fail to see who is behind you. Who it is that has made ways for you and who yet hides your shame and fears.

Just as behind every King you find a Queen and various advisors, behind every leader you will find advisors, confidants and friends. Yet you brag that all of your achievements have been at your hand.

You cannot fool me, because I know who has opened doors for you and even closed many behind you to protect you from danger. I know who groomed and supported you when you was alone, afraid and crying. You and I know who keep you going daily and who lay you down to sleep. The who that has loved you so greatly and you in turn destroyed. I know who you have deeply injured and who you desperately fear. Most of all, I know who can help you and erase all of your fears.

Yes the world sees only you, but you know the whole truth. Without the who behind you, you would never have made it this far. So when you get besides yourself, try to remember why you are. Maybe then you will stop stepping on those who helped you along thus far.

AN EXCUSE FOR RACISM

Now day's people seem to have an excuse for just about everything. They call the misdeeds of others illnesses in an attempt to excuse their misdeeds. Tell me, what is the excuse for racism?

As children we are taught what to believe, how to act and react by parents and those around us. As we age wisdom should take over, seeing that we become responsible for our actions, reactions and beliefs.

No longer can any of us excuse racism by blaming others for our behavior. That's not to say that other individual's actions cannot influence us to distrust and feel ill towards them and others of that nationality. However, in the end we are responsible for our actions.

Racism is not an inherited physical or mental illness, but it is a premeditated weapon of choice that is used by racist to spread their poison to others.

In 2008, let us work together that true change may come about. We can join our children in embracing others or they will do it alone.

JUSTICE BLINDERS

Justice wears blinders, because she that is governed by he cannot stand to see the twists that are placed on the laws that were adopted to create just decisions. She is not blind, but has been incased in justice's ice. Just ice has become her name, in that she cannot feel any fires of rightness.

Laws they say are formulated to serve victims, but we see that victims are often further victimized. Even when they can prove their innocence, lawmakers sometimes force them to pay a portion of the fines and just for revenue sake. They also often convict by who you are, who you know or your race. In many cases pedophiles and wife abusers stand a better chance of not getting convicted than many who are innocent.

Justice cannot of herself act, when unjust men and women continue to write unjust laws, that are then carried out by unjust justices. Would to God that men could see, then possible they would remove the blinders that have been placed on justice's eyes.

PARASITE

The enemy that lives within and feed on your insides in an attempt to get out and destroy others. Its very being depends on your support, since it cannot of itself survive. It cries hungry, hungry whenever someone approaches. It is aggressive in pursuing its sustenance, ravenous as wolves and sinister in nature. It is persistent in its attempts to destroy souls, as one that reproduces evil, and more infectious than AIDS. It is so stubborn that the strongest antibiotics cannot cure its host. It is temperamental, eager to destroy and nocturnal in nature.

This night creature is a predator that nibbles at its prey until the host has become terminal. In the end the outer shell of the victim will crumble as the parasite leap to its next victim.

No amount of reasoning will stop a parasite. Its end must be swift and its remains incinerated with fire.

Be very careful, for when you least expect, you may find that you are the temple of this most vile and deceitful creature known as a parasite.

Note: Be very careful of "The Company That You Keep."

LYING LIPS AND QUIVERING HIPS

Lying lips and quivering hips have much in common. Both will do whatever it takes to gain what they want. Lying lips and quivering hips ruin families, nations and chances for a better future. While lying lips give orders that shape and reshape the lives of those they were set to protect, quivering hips commit acts that shape and reshape the lives of those they promised to love, cherish, honor and protect.

These lips have a life of their own. They operate under a form of rightness, but are marked by deceit. Their objective is to deceive gullible listeners who have failed to be educated outside of what they see, hear, taste, touch and can smell. People whose inner warning system called common sense is being ignored or has been deactivated, thereby turning off their spiritual guide. These ignore the inner child that can yet hear the voice of God, see through pure eyes with clarity and feel his tug at their hearts.

Laughter flies from their lips as the unsuspecting fall prey to their games. The school of hard knocks has nothing on them, since they fail to learn lessons taught. People with lying lips continue to repeat evil words, commit evil deeds and spew out messages that drip with deceit. They wrap listeners in webs of uncertainty and cause them to believe that they are the givers of life instead of being the bringers of death. These lips speak from the depths of those that have been deceived and seek to deceive others.

While the wise; those gifted with discernment can read their movements, those lacking wisdom will challenge the wise calling them liars. Later their victims learn that they too have fallen prey to those lying lips and quivering hips.

You see, quivering hips gyrate pleasure at the expense of others. Fools sit staring at them, while waiting to pay for a communicable disease.

What a mess those do what I want to, whenever I want to and to whomever I want to lying lips make.

I ask, where were you when Lying Lips and Quivering Hips 101 was being taught? Why didn't you listen when the lesson was being taught? Now you have to suffer the consequences that "Lying Lips and Quivering Hips" delivers.

Those who fail to study God's words will not see warning signs. They will miss turns, fall prey to false prophets and leaders who are themselves lost. Fooled they are by smooth talk, slick dress and those with fake credentials, who lie about their status and abilities. Check their backgrounds and you will see what big liars they are.

Stop falling for forms of rightness and look deep that you may see the enemy waiting to strike you down. Don't be fooled by those with "Lying Lips and Quivering Hips."

LYING LIPS
and
QUIVERING HIPS

THINGS THAT CAN DESTROY

Betrayals, indiscretions and even withholding information are all "Things That Can Destroy." Secrets, appendages and deceptions if allowed all can destroy lives. Whispers coming from lying lips and those building road blocks that cause others to stumble and fall, all are "Things That Can Destroy." Don't allow "Things That Can Destroy" to take control of your mind, heart and mouth.

Individuals are known by what they do as well as what they say. Believe it or not, people reap what they sow and hidden iniquities are revealed. Lies no matter the size your mind perceive them, are "Things That Can Destroy."

It never cease to amaze me how people who voice their undying love for another and brag about their self-control, allow that small appendage between their legs or the one housed in their mouths to ruin lives.

This small appendage runs everywhere, poking its head in and out of any and everything that will allow it entrance. Just like a Cobra snake it charms and deceives. I won't hurt or get you pregnant, just allow me in the back door or just a little head will do. Now you lay in some Hospice Care Facility, because you allowed wrinkled up "Things That Can Destroy" to make a fool out of you.

These small things cannot even clean themselves, yet these small germ ridden appendages have been allowed to control your body and mind.

People this is real life; not some "Burger King" slogan where you get to "Have it your way." There are repercussions for our actions and inactions. Close your legs girls, pull up your zipper boys and keep your mouth off private places. Don't ruin your life by becoming prey to "Things That Can Destroy."

NEVER TRUST A SHARK

In or out of water never trust a shark. Its sharp teeth can rip you from throat to stern.

Card sharks, loan sharks, stock market sharks and even sales sharks lurk in the dark. As do little sharks, big sharks, shrewd sharks and want to be sharks. Then you have salt water sharks, fresh water sharks, sharks with suits and some with dresses also lurking in the dark.

Color matters not, for sharks come in different colors and strike when you least expect. If caught in their grasp, you will surely come to harm.

My advice is to "NEVER TRUST A SHARK."

GENOCIDE BY LOWER WAGES AND TAXATION

Genocide by lower wages and TAXATION are tools that can surely bring you down. While you fight to make ends meet, your dreams go unrealized.

Often we are so busy trying to make a living that we cannot become who God has designed us to be. Many of us are overworked and underpaid, leading to inward and outward struggles.

Believe me when I say, that there is more than one way to destroy a people and a nation. Genocide by lower wages and high taxes, give you the ability to gain their lands, break their spirits and cause their demise. If you take away their ability to sustain themselves and their families, even their dignity will suffer.

Over tax a community that has little or no commercial tax base and you will strip the residents of their homes. Floating bond after bond to expand where expansions are not necessary or sought by most area residents, all can cause a communities demise. This is what happens when greed takes over.

Pee pie, I see you and I know what you are doing. I know that the one square mile of Roosevelt, Long Island is on high demand. With little to no commercial base, we will pay these escalating taxes until we cannot afford to pay them anymore. Then you will swoop down like a vulture on its prey and take the spoils. Some people don't believe that "fat meat is greasy" until it's too late.

I say, shame, shame, shame on you.

POISON
(PEOPLE OPENLY ISSUING,
SPEWING ODIOUS NOTHINGS)

Vile, venomous vaunting by men and women who themselves are replete of God's love. These vain, mean spirited, angry people find pleasure at the expense of tearing at the inners of others. Rotted insides and poisonous veins that drip with deceit describe them. Envious of everyone and everything, they claim that life has passed them bye. However, they have chosen to use their energy to spew poison against others. Maybe their lives would be fulfilled if goodness was their aim. Now they sit rotting as they age. Little hope is seen as the days of their lives go bye. So they sit and criticize others, calling others nothing, when the reality is that poisonous people are venomous and vile. They are often old, bitter and good for nothing but spewing evil. They are outcasts that are trying to gather other foolish souls to their stinking way of thinking. The end for all that walk in their door is destruction.

Run away from people who openly issue odious nothings or someone may describe you too as a poisonous person.

EVIL COMMUNICATION CORRUPTS

Believe what you want to, but evil communication does corrupt good manner. I don't care how nice you are, how pretty or brilliant, if you hang with bullies, liars, thieves and the likes, you will began to take on their characteristics. You will become comfortable in things that once caused you discomfort.

Disobeying your parents and those in authority will become second nature to you as will lying. Your sense of judgment will become warped and you will fall into trouble. If you don't change your company and way of living; you will get into trouble and that trouble could destroy your future and/or your life.

Light bulb moment; God and family are usually the only ones that you can count on to be concerned about your best interest. Also, there is no such thing as a little lie or little white lie. Lies don't come in color and are not clean because they are termed "white." A lie is just that, a lie.

Anyone who cloaks you in doing wrong or cover up your wrong is not a friend. While some people will benefit from a second and even third chance, most people who commit crimes don't learn from their mistakes.

I'm not saying that you should not give them a chance to redirect their lives, but if they continue this negative behavior and all other avenues have been exhausted, bring them up on charges. Some people have to go up to grow up. They have to go to the big house to see what it is really like, because they only believe what they see.

Understand also, that those who love you must sometimes make hard and painful decisions when they are attempting to save you. Often the pain that you experience from your own bad choices cannot compare to the pain that you cause your loved ones. Those who really love you are willing to suffer with you in order to restore you. They understand that for some people, lessons can only be learned through adversity and pain.

My advice to all of us is to acknowledge our wrongs, change what is necessary and pay for our actions. Best of all change the company you keep, the places you go and your manner of communicating with others.

Know also that a real friend will be straight with you even if it means risking your anger and the friendship. A friend will tell you when you are wrong and encourage you to do right. Why, because they want what is best for you.

It never ceases to amaze me, how grown we all feel when we are young. Often we commit wrong acts and fail to understand the repercussions. Our youth somehow make us feel that we cannot be prosecuted. We puff out our chest for others to "see me; I'm bad baby." As soon as we get caught, we call for our mama. Even many adult criminals start whining for mommy.

If most people would listen and learn from those having their best interest at heart, they would not be in the predicament they are in today. Learning right behavior as young adults and following it can save your life. Further, it will serve you well, because "Evil Communication Corrupts."

I HEARD YOU

Yeah, I heard you. You thought I didn't or thought that I forgot, but I heard you. I heard you when you said, "I don't get mad, I get even." Yeah, I heard you loud and clear.

I heard you. You thought I didn't or that I forgot, but I heard you when you said, "I'm a Christian." Yeah, I heard you loud and clear.

Actions speak louder than words and yours say that you are not a Christian but a fake. I don't doubt that you are religious, but that isn't the same as being a Christian. Yeah, I heard you and soon others will too. Then your reputation will be nothing and not those you attempt to destroy.

Yeah, I heard you. You thought I didn't or thought that I forgot, but I heard you talking about me to others. Yeah, I heard you loud and clear.

Yeah, I heard you and so did God. I'm not your worry, but baby he is. Yeah, I heard you loud and clear. More than that, I see you too and what you say just doesn't match your actions.

THE NEIGHBORHOOD

Our young men need to become more like men of the "Wood" instead of "Boyz In The Hood." Our young ladies need to learn how to work "together" and not be out "to-get-her."

Don't be intimidated by people who tease you because you choose to use proper English when speaking. Also, when they accuse you of thinking that you are better than they are; know that it is their inferiority complex that has caused their problems and not you.

There is nothing fashionable or professional about loud talking, gum smacking, neck snapping and speaking in grunts. Further, why would anyone attempt to glamorize the misuse of the "English" language by explaining it away as "Ebonics?" The African American vernacular is not "Ebonics." As diverse people, most of us can switch in and out of humor. We know when we can be comedians and when we must speak with intelligence.

A perfect example of this is seen in Tyler Perry's works. He knows what forum to use humor in and when to turn it off. After all, we are a Multi-dialect, multi-colloquial and voice shifting people.

Marcus Garvy, Malcolm X, Dr. Martin Luther King, Jr., Mrs. Rosa Parks, Representative Shirley Chisholm, Frederick Douglas nor Senator Barbra Jordan resorted to using broken sentences and what is now termed "Ebonics & Ghetto language" in addressing others. What about Nelson Mandela, Dr. Maya Angelou or Chris Gardner ("The Pursuit of Happiness")? Perhaps they are trying to be White too.

We need to think about what we do and say. Think about how our words and actions affect our young people. Years ago, many of our mothers and fathers could not attend school, but had to work to feed the family. Some never learned to read and write, but they sought better for their children. Today many parents don't encourage their children to speak proper English. They further handicap their children in naming them. Then you get angry when school mates tease them about their no names or employers refuse to hire them due to their lack of verbal skills.

Then some that apply for a professional position show up for the interview with blue, green or red hair. Many are unable to complete a job application, while others sit in the interview popping gum, inappropriately dressed and snapping at the interviewer.

Minorities who refuse to speak "Ebonics" are often looked at as "uppity negroes" or worse.

After completing the eighth grade in the then segregated Montgomery, Alabama, I went on to earn my G.E.D. in New York, and earned an Associates Degree in Business Administration. In Alabama I was taught by all Black teachers and they never spoke or taught us to speak "Ebonics." Furthermore, a Southern twang or country accent is not "Ebonics." It is the language that our people have mastered over the years; a language that our African, Indian, Colored and Caucasian relatives use so eloquently.

Don't get angry at me and say they I think that I am better than you, because I refuse to come down to your level of speaking. It is lowering standards like it or not.

Believe me when I say, that I yet struggle with the English language, because I missed so much by not attending high school. I have ears to hear and eyes to read books that help me do better. You are not being asked to be perfect in your speech, but to prosper in this world, it is essential that you learn and speak proper English.

I urge you to attach yourself to people that are doing positive things. Watch what they do and how they do it. Learn from their good and from their mistakes. Watch positive programs, listen to positive music and emulate positive acts that you may become a positive person.

THE TRUTH ABOUT TITHE PAYING

Most of our lives we have been taught that we rob God if we don't pay tithes. In most churches we are beat over the head on Sundays with Malachi 3:7-12.

Many of us have lost our homes, neglected our children and lost good spouses as we attempted to follow the directives of church pastors. From pulpits they crack their whips and demand that we tithe at God's command.

We believe them and pay tithes in Jesus name. In the meantime our families are suffering and we fall into distress instead of being blessed.

I remember Mother Brayboy, who kept telling me what 1 Timothy 5:8 said; "But if any provide not for his own, and specially for those of his own house, he hath denied the faith, and is worse than an infidel." I was conflicted. It wasn't that I didn't believe her or God's word, but I found myself being more concerned about pleasing the pastor. He would call you to the front of the church and embarrass you in front of other parishioners and even visitors.

After years of paying tithes with a troubled spirit, God has extricated me from the demands of man by showing me the truth. What he has done for me, I will now share with you.

One day to my surprise I heard the following words, "Show me in the Bible where my Son paid tithes." "You said that he is your perfect example, then show me where he paid tithes."

Not being cognizant that God was addressing me, I picked up my Bible, started flipping the pages while telling him about when Jesus paid taxes/tribute. God quickly reminded me that he said tithes and not taxes/tribute. Then the teacher took me to school.

He took me to the tax/tribute issue. He asked me whose superscription was on the money. I answered Caesar's. He reminded me of what Jesus had said when the "Pharisees took counsel how they might entangle him in his talk." Verse 16, "They sent out unto him their disciples with Herodians, saying Master, we know that thou art true, and teachest the way of God in truth, neither carest thou for any man: for thou regardest not the person of men."

They asked him "What thinkist thou? Is it lawful to give tribute unto Caesar, or not?" Verse 18, "But Jesus perceived their wickedness, and said, why tempt ye me, ye hypocrites?" In verse 19 Jesus said, "Show me the tribute money, and they brought unto him a penny." Verse 20 "And he saith unto them, Whose is this image and superscription?" Verse 21, "They say unto him, Caesar's. Then saith he unto them, Render (give) therefore unto Caesar the things which are Caesar's and unto God the things that are God's."

I was told to turn to Malachi. Once there, he opened my eyes that I may see and my heart that I may be receptive to his words of revelation.

Allow me to share with you, what the teacher taught me that day. He used the scriptures as they were and didn't change a word verse by verse.

First of all Malachi 3:7-12 in the KJV states the following:

Verse 7, "Even from the days of your fathers ye are gone away from mine ordinances, and have not kept them. Return unto me, and I will return unto you, saith the Lord of hosts. But ye said, Wherein shall we return?"

Verse 8, "Will a man rob God? Yet ye have robbed me. But ye say, Wherein have we robbed thee? In tithes and offerings."

Verse 9, "Ye are cursed with a curse: for ye have robbed me, even this whole nation."

Verse 10, "Bring ye all the tithes into the storehouse, that there may be meat in mine house, and prove me now herewith, saith the Lord of hosts, if I will not open you the windows of heaven, and pour you out a blessing, that there shall not be room enough to receive it."

Verse 11, "And I will rebuke the devourer for your sakes, and he shall not destroy the fruits of your ground; neither shall your vine cast her fruit before the time in the field, saith the Lord of hosts."

Verse 12, "And all nations shall call you blessed: for ye shall be a delightsome land, saith the Lord of hosts."

As it relates to verse "7," God reminded me that he was speaking to his children, the Israelites. Further, he reminded me, that the Gentiles were considered Heathen (an offensive term used to describe those who don't believe in the God of the Bible) and had not been grafted into God's family at that time. Then God asked me, "How could I have been talking to you?" He pointed out that in verses "8-10," his usage of the word "ye" was singular. He was speaking to the children of Israel as one unit.

He further said that when he asked the question of them, "Will a man rob God," it wasn't to get a response from them, but that he was chastening, teaching and reminding them of their duties under the law. They were hard headed and constantly disobeyed the laws of God. This is seen throughout the Bible.

Keep in mind, that from Genesis through Malachi, they were under the "law and the prophets." Grace and truth; a better and more perfect way came by Jesus the Christ in the New Testament (Matthew through Revelations), as did the Gentiles being grafted into the family of God. Prior to this time, we were considered an unclean and Heathen people.

God told the Israelites that they robbed him in tithes and offerings and the penalty was, being "cursed with a curse," "even this whole nation." Verse 9. His usage of "ye" was in speaking to the Israelites, as was the term this whole nation.

In Verse 10, They were instructed to "Bring ye all the tithes into the storehouse, that there may be meat in mine house, and prove me now herewith, saith the Lord of hosts, if I will not open you (Israel) the windows of heaven, and pour you (Israel) out a blessing, that there shall not be room enough to receive it."

Then in Verse 11, God pointed out that He said, "And I will rebuke the devourer for your (Israel's) sakes, and he shall not destroy the fruits of your (Israel's) ground; neither shall your vine cast her fruit before the time in the field, saith the Lord of hosts."

People we are not mentioned until Verse 12, where he said, "And all nations shall call you (Israel) blessed: for ye shall be a delightsome land, saith the Lord of hosts." That was to again distinguish God's children and tell them if they obeyed the law, he would bless them to the point that all nations would look on them and see how blessed they were, because they served him.

I was admittedly confused as to why all of these years' preachers have been misleading parishioners. I asked God, "Then is it wrong to pay tithes?" He said, "no if you are operating under the law and the prophets." Further he reminded me that he gave us the right of choice and that "It is not necessary for those who walk under grace and truth."

He reminded me of Romans 8:3, which says, "For what the law could not do in that it was weak through the flesh, God sending his own son in the likeness of sinful flesh, and for sin, condemned sin in the flesh."

Oh yes, he let me know that some preachers would say that I took one verse of a scripture and ran with it and that's not what God meant. He had something for that in Romans 3:3-4, "For what if some did not believe? Shall their unbelief make the faith of God without effect? God forbid: yea, let God be true, but every man a liar; as it is written. That thou mightest be justified in the saying, and mightest overcome when thou art judged." God also reminded me that we know and see in part, but when he comes all will be revealed.

Then he took me back to the tax (tribute) again and asked me whose superscription was on that money? I said, "Caesar's." He said again to "Render (give) therefore unto Caesar the things which are Caesar's and unto God the things that are God's." Whose pictures are on most of our money; dead Presidents.

I asked God, "Then what do You want from me, since the cattle on a thousand hills are yours and you don't need my money?" He reminded me of Romans 12:1 "I BESEECH you therefore brethren, by the mercies of God, that ye present your bodies a living sacrifice, holy, acceptable unto God, which is your reasonable service." At your convenience study the chapters spoken of in these passages.

My father is awesome! He reminded me of what Paul the Apostle said in 2 Corinthians 9:6-7 when instructing the church brethren in collecting bounty (fees). "But this I say, he which soweth sparingly shall reap sparingly; and he which soweth bountifully shall reap also bountifully. Every man according as he purpose in his heart, so let him give, not grudgingly or of necessity; for God loveth a cheerful giver." Man may not care about the spirit in which you give but God does. We are to give as he has blessed us to give.

This information was not revealed to me to bash churches, but to free me of the tug of war in my spirit.

You see, whenever I gave tithes or refused to give the amount pastors demanded, often they would quote 1 Timothy 5:8, "You are worse than an infidel and have denied the faith, if you don't take care your own, especially they of your own household." They considered the church your household, and not your spouse, children, an elderly or widowed parent.

I have learned that you can twist the scriptures to mean just about anything, but if you want and seek truth, God will speak truth into your spirit. Believe me when I tell you that was some "a haw" moment for me.

I felt so bad, for I had been giving out of necessity. My children had been sleeping on the floor, my underwear filled with holes and we walked while my pastor had three cars. Knowing my condition and that my children and I had been put out of our home by my husband for his mistress, this man bled me dry and I allowed it.

The pastor's appreciation offerings were at the tune of $250. per person in your household and this in the 1970's. You were *expected to give how much the pastor and staff told you to give when he went to State, District and National meetings. If you didn't, you were berated in front of everyone. We were even charged for elaborate appreciations as many are today.*

There was more money being spent by parishioners on appreciation services, pastors and their families than money being spent to care for parishioners own families. While offerings were taken for pastors' children's birthdays and college, nothing was being taken up for other children in the church. Mostly this was due to people being under the influence of these pastors teachings for years. Others were intimidated by them and in fear of these pastors. After all they were said to be the watchmen on the wall for parishioners' souls.

Oh, the "hen is coming home to roost", seeing that "judgment must first begin at the household of faith, and if it begin with us, where shall the end be for those that don't believe?"

All the time that you are giving at their rate, you are finding yourselves further and further in debt. Then when your rent is due and your baby is out of milk and diapers, they say, "I'm praying for you sister or God bless you sister." Why don't you bless me, since you have my money? The answer usually is "That's church money; God's money."

Some even encourage you to give your last and tell you that by the next day, God will replace it some 10, some 20 and others a hundred fold.

Tears are forming in my eyes. How stupid I had been and what had I done to my children? My husband was giving the pastor whatever he wanted financially although he was no longer a member of the church. Also I was giving them almost all that

I had, including helping pay for the church building and new furniture.

Oh what a revelation from God. Then he reminded me of the widow's mite and what it meant to him. He told me that his children know his voice and a stranger they will not follow. All of a sudden I realized that I had been following the dictates of man and had not been following God.

I apologize dear God and thank you for not letting me die before I got back on track. I apologize my children for not listening to Mother Brayboy who tried diligently to get me to change my way. I apologize for the hurt many of you will feel after reading this, but I hope it free you as it did me.

Then I asked God, "What do I say to pastors who call me on the carpet and say that I don't know what I am talking about?" He answered me like this; "For what if some did not believe? Shall their unbelief make the faith of God without effect? God forbid: yea, let God be true, but every man a liar; as it is written, That thou mightest be justified in thy saying, and mightest overcome when thou art judged." Romans 3:3-4 KJV

Then God said, "And fear not them which kill the body, but are not able to kill the soul: but rather fear me (him) who is able to destroy your soul and body in Hell." Matthew 10:28 Then I read verses 27 "What I tell you in darkness that speak ye in light: and what ye hear in the ear, preach ye upon the house tops."

The conflict is not in God's word, but mankind's interpretation of it and their greed. While some clergy members genuinely don't know that tithe paying for years now has not been a requirement, I believe that most know. They won't tell their congregations because they fear losing money. Some are not confident that their parishioners will continue to give at their current levels, therefore they give half truths mixed in lies from the pulpit.

I suggest that you obey the word of God and give as God has blessed you to give. Not grudgingly (angry because you are being forced to do it through embarrassment; having your name called out) or by necessity (demanding specific amounts of money).

Don't allow others to make a fool out of you by believing that God instructed them to say that 20 people in the room can give $1,000., and no one can leave until we get it. God never told them to have you give a specific amount and God did not instruct them that he would return it to you at a rate of 10, 20 or 100 fold by tomorrow.

To add insult to the injury that is already being done, some churches now have ATM machines on their premises. They play on people's emotions when they are most vulnerable. This is an answer for those who leave most of their money at home. Your Debit, Master Card, Visa and the like will do.

How low can they go? I say, lower than the floor in this case.

What is wrong with God's people?! Why do many of us believe man before God?

Give as God has blessed you to be able to give. Be honest and do it with joy that God be glorified and your lives are blessed.

Remember also that "Vengeance" is the Lord's and not ours. We cannot use what they have done as an excuse, or to give us permission to become like them.

Always remember that neither money nor paying tithes can purchase you a place around God's throne. He wants you. Also *keep in mind, that people of God will give from their hearts when the church is in need. Don't allow anyone to use the "widow's mite" scripture or any other scripture to trick you into giving.*

Remember loved ones, that if you lack wisdom, ask God who give to all generously and without berating.

THE GOLDEN LEASH

Bridled, restrained and held back are words that I hear when the word leash is said. Brilliance, wealth and status are words that come to mind when golden is uttered. When these words are put together they become a form of restraint laced in brilliance.

"The Golden Leash" is not just any old leash, but God extends it. Blessing and salvation driven it is. It is not a bond of slavery but a line of restraint that keeps you from destruction. While its brilliance and radiance speaks of its value, its grip serves to keep you connected to God that he may keep you from harm.

As a bridle is used to guide and keep the horse in line, "The Golden Leash" is needed to keep our tongues from destroying others and ourselves.

"The Golden Leash" will gently pull at you when you are going too far with your words, actions and thoughts. It can also be used to jerk you back from the fires of life when you fail to take heed to its friendly nudge. It will also help you bridle your tongue when you are under attack by lying lips and will help you stay the course when quivering hips come your way.

Be thankful for "The Golden Leash," for it is salvation driven. Also keep in mind that it is a safety valve and not a control mechanism.

NO CONSCIOUS SOUL OR FEAR

From the depth of their souls are seen dark pools of anger swelling and rising. Where did it come from, what caused it, how will it appease itself and who will become its next victim?

Without thought, without knowing, without fear or concern it strikes. It throws blow by blow to the body of its victims. As black blood began to flow, excitement rise and laughter, demonic laughter is heard by angels. Eyes darkened from loss of consciousness, stare back at us. Hells' scorching fires have seared them. One by one sweet angels fall, leaving lost souls that have been deserted by parents, clergy, teachers and family with little or no hope.

The bells are tolling, who will be next? Will it be your son, daughter, grandchild or one of mine? Who can stop them and how? Who has failed them and why?

Things have replaced love and attention. We have become my thing rules and me. It's my time you say, while leaving your offspring to roam the mean streets. Drugs, parties, men, women and a good time have replaced quality time by parents, family values and prayer.

Street gangs, bad asses and the undisciplined influence our young. Then you wonder why they turn and spill your blood. You left them to the streets and you showed them coldness. It was you who failed to love them like good parents should. Even many churches have failed them, since no money is being collected from them. So do not cry and scream, when you stand and watch the Universe's justice on those that kill, injure and destroy. After all, without love to guide them, many have "No Conscious Soul or Fear."

GETTING OVER IT

Early one Sunday morning I heard these words coming out of my television set, "Get over it!" I took offense with the arrogant manner in which it was spoken. This pastor spoke of sexual abuse suffered by many as children at the hands of the clergy. He attempted to soften the blow by saying he understood what victims had gone through. Instead that person had served to deepen the wounds already inflicted.

Although he has since died, his words have left a scar on many hearts. A few callous words repeated over and over again, will be what many listeners remember instead of all the good he has done.

How dare anyone who has not experienced what you or I have, casually say get over it? Your status in life does not give you the right to further injure others in such a callous manner.

Get over it, you say. Well, when you can demonstrate to me that you have gotten over the same tragedies that I have experienced in my life, then maybe, I will accept your words of "Get over it." Possibly I can then believe it, because you have accomplished the feat.

Get over it? Anyone who has experienced what the rejected, ejected, broken and I have experienced would not with arrogance callously say, "Get over it." Instead they would say that you can overcome it.

No stroking is necessary, but decorum is appreciated. Did you ask why use the words overcome it and not get over it? You say they mean the same thing? Do you understand tact and offense?

Although offenses will come, I believe it has added to it, "Woe" to the man by which the offense comes.

Telling one to overcome it speaks to strength, power and endurance, while get over it denotes a know it all attitude, lack of understanding and pure arrogance.

Juvenile behavior would cause me to flip you the bird when you tell me to "Get over it," but for the grace of God. Then I will hear nothing else you say, but instead listen to those who have learned that by his grace and through mercy we can overcome the it in our lives.

Today I say to each of you, that together and not separate, we can overcome obstacles.

RELIGIOUSITY

Have you ever been struck by a religious bullet? You know the kind that claimers of Christianity use. One side of their mouth drips the words of Christianity and the other deceit and destruction.

These claimers of Christianity are locked and loaded with religiosity. They say trust me, but look into their eyes and you will see a manipulator, liar and wolf attempting to hide in sheep's clothing.

Beware I say of religious people, for even their form of godliness is warped and their facade cannot hold them steady.

Religious people are everywhere and come from different cultures and backgrounds. They are male, female, heterosexual, bisexual, homosexual and asexual. Their color, shape and race also differ. They talk the part, but at every opportunity seek whom they may destroy. Disagree with them and your butt is out of luck. Watch out, they have locked and loaded their religious gun to fire on and destroy you.

These people failed the Christian test. They may know the word but failed to know God and yield themselves to his teachings. They dress the part, but sit in the seat of the scornful, have corruptible power and a form of godliness. Their armor is full of chinks and not able to stand up to the whole armor of God.

These use their illusions of power to fool the gullible and turn them against those hand picked by God to make a difference. I say, "different day, similar people with the same beliefs."

Locked and loaded they are, but every shot fired will enter them, every hole dug will bury them and every evil work has been written in the "BOOKS" for Judgment Day.

Be thankful for religiosity, for it will help Christians grow, test your armor and sharpen your sight. It will move you to a quiet space, make you pray for others and pray that you not fall into temptation. It will make you smile and sorrowful at the same time. Smile, because you know that you already have the victory through Jesus and sorrowful because you know that God's judgment will fall on them.

I say to you all, "There is a place between Black and White, right and wrong, religiosity and Christianity. It is the place that I call "Shaded Hues;" the place where the unscrupulous walk.

Do not adopt or adapt to religiosity, but hold to Christianity that God keep you from evil when faced with evil. Choose this day who you will serve. Will it be God or Satan?

DOWNS AND UPS

If you fail to master downs, you will certainly fail at ups. For it is downs that develop character, that our remembrance not fail us. While ups are often plagued by forgetfulness, downs can bring back painful memories. These downs help keep us humble, that ups not cause our demise.

Too often those in positions of power, forget who they really are. They forget that the power they have acquired came with the position, and will remain behind when they are gone. If they accepted this, just maybe they would stop flexing the muscles they no longer have and stop the huffing and puffing before their own house fall down.

Tick tock, tick tock, time is almost up. Fighting is divisive and further shortening the days. "Hickory Dickory Dock, the mouse ran up the clock. The clock struck one, the mouse ran down! Hickory Dickory Dock. Hickory Dickory Dock, the mouse ran up the clock, the clock struck noon," he's here too soon! Hillary, Dick and Dobbs.

Take care for it is the people, who can soften or harden a fall. If you fail the people, you may become elected then rejected that the rejected be elected.

WHAT HAVE WE BECOME
ROYAL PEOPLE

Many men, women and children have died that those referred to as Colored, Negroes or Blacks may be free. They came from the North, South, East and West. They were not only Black Americans but Asians and Caucasians alike. Many were beat, dragged, lynched and imprisoned by the same Caucasians that beat and lynched people of color. Others had hoses and dogs turned on them by lawmakers who were lawbreakers.

These days many people of color are their own worst enemy. Young and old minorities are killing, maiming, raping and robbing their own. The disrespect level against both sexes is steadily increasing. Women are referred to as bitches and worst. Even our seniors are not excluded from this madness.

Then males add insult to injury by demanding our women give them blow jobs. When they do it in an attempt to hold on to them, these scandalous males deride them in public. Somehow they managed to forget that they took her virginity. Then instead of covering her shame they announce it to the world.

I dare ask you "brothers," why not cover your sisters' shame and stop displaying her half naked body for money? Why not become their teachers and supporters instead of turning them on to such negative programs as "Girls gone wild?" Help them learn to display good values, instead of encouraging them to gap their legs and display their nakedness. Oh, but you didn't stop there, you pawned her off to your friends after introducing her to drugs. Now she has no idea who fathered her child or where the AIDS that is ravaging her body came from. "What Have We Become Royal People" and what did our ancestors fight and die for?

We need to stop emulating the negative behaviors of those around us, who will do anything for money and fame. Think of the future you are preparing for your daughters and sons. Mothers do you want your daughters and sons to be like you if your behavior is negative? Fathers, do you want your daughters to fall prey to males like the sons you are raising to disrespect women bodies?

Fathers stop lauding your sons for their sexual prowess and train them to be men. Teach them to care where they plant their seed and to support the children of their loins. Teach them that having sex requires great responsibility.

Women are more than a piece of meat, to be used to satisfy some males' insatiable appetite for sex. Men should not allow themselves to be reduced to an uncontrolled organ, where their only function is to gain physical pleasure by any means.

Teach these young men to ask themselves prior to having sex with a young lady, "Is this the woman that I am marrying or am I taking her home to meet my parents?" Ask yourself, "Do I really want to trade my life for a fleeting feeling?" Furthermore, if she is "the one," then what is the rush?

We need to teach our daughters to think with their heads and not their hearts. Tell her the truth; that if he loves her, he will marry her instead of pressing for sex? Further, women need to ask themselves, if this man will love, honor and respect me or is he only interested in sex?

Have you watched to see how he treats the women in his family and women around him? Men, have you watched to see if she respects her mother and those around her? When his or her parents say stay home, do they sneak out anyway? These are things that signal problems and speak to their inability to follow directions, even when not agreed with.

Mothers stop allowing your sons to do what you don't allow your girls to do. Teach your sons responsibility and stop telling them that when they get a young lady pregnant, it is her parents' problem or let welfare care for them. It is all our problems.

What happened to love songs and holding her tenderly as you danced and called her your Queen? What happened to your honor as men and how did you fall so low? Why has her protector now become her enemy and why do you hate her so? Is it because you hate the very skin that you are in or maybe you hate the woman who bare you?

Where has genuine love and concern for them gone and the love that real men of old gave to their women? Why can't you help them see the value in themselves by showing them by example their beauty, instead of seeking their booty?

Have you forgotten where that one rib came from? It was taken out of you, that you would understand the value in her, love her as you do yourselves and protect her. Instead you have gone from "A One In A Million You," "You Are My Lady," "When A Man Loves A Woman" and "Three Times A Lady" to songs of degradation.

Even our mother of the Civil Rights Movement, Mrs. Rosa Parks, was assaulted and by a Black man. "What Have We Become Royal People" and what did they die for oh people of mine?

Have our own now become the animals that we once despised? Wake up, wake up America! Yes in 2008, many are moving backward instead of stepping forward.

I find that the hands that were made to comfort me are being used to strangle the life out of me, hold me down while you and your boys run a train on me and beat me until I am bloody. Even the mouth that should speak wisdom and peace to me now call me a bitch! "What Have We Become Royal People," that we now fear our own?

Young women as well as young men are in the game. Gang bangers, drug abusers, rapist and murderers have taken over. We that carried them in our loins gave birth to them or cared for them thus far, are too afraid to put them in check. Instead of turning them in for committing crimes, many live off the spoils of their crimes. Again I ask, "What Have We Become Royal People" and what did our ancestors fight and die for?

Bullies, thieves and destroyers of our future are running rampant. Deceivers, liars and back biters too. Lawmakers that are lawbreakers and even many sitting in pulpits. Even the hoary heads have huddled together in teaching the young to gossip and hate others. They devalue life and anyone that accomplishes anything positive. Their inadequacies have lead them to bitterness as they watch their dreams slip away. Anyone good become a threat to them. Envy and jealously eat at their inners and eventually decay their souls. They know that they are doomed and introduce the unwise to their stinking way of thinking. They will fight to the end to take the foolish with them as Satan does with his fall.

The unwise fail to see that they are nothing but a means to the deceivers end. Thou fool, you are being used to hurl rocks on their behalf and even at your own. They don't like you, but use you to elevate themselves. Their fear has moved them to take any measure to win as they feel their power slipping away. These types lie their way to the top, not knowing that they are headed for a fall. With one foot on a "banana peel" and the other one sliding them to Hell, they gather to themselves company to go with them. "What Have We Become Royal People" of mine and what did our ancestors fight and die for?

Fools try to amass power and by any means. They fail to understand that true power comes from God and cannot be purchased or duplicated. They have been deceived and in turn deceive others. They are the blind that lead the blind to destruction.

"Power corrupts and absolute power corrupts absolutely" I have learned. Great responsibility comes with it and that most people cannot handle. What again I ask, "What Have We Become Royal People?"

All of us need to take a good look at the prisons and grave yards that are being filled with our children. We need to teach our children God's rules for living peaceful, because in these days life means nothing to many. Our children are lined up against walls and fences then slaughtered like animals. Not just rogue cops, but you of color in your own neighborhoods. Again, I ask you, "What Have We Become Royal People" and what did our ancestors fight and die for?

Lacking understanding, many have walked away from God, seeing themselves as the suppliers of their wealth. Little do they know that they have fallen prey to the fool's way of thinking. While they serve money and even purchase churches run by men, they fail to see that salvation is not in men but of God.

Separation is the flavor of the day and unity by clan only. The joke is on you, because we all came from one Earthly mother and father named Adam and Eve. More than this, we came from God.

While many that are my color have immigrated to America or came through immigrants, it amaze me how many hate those considered Black Americans. From street corners, working establishments, churches and neighborhoods it is rampant. I say that the pot is not greater than the kettle or the clay the potter.

Instead of fighting one-another we need to take our young people back to where honor and strength abide. Take them to the place where people worked for what they wanted and did without if they could not afford the "it."

Teach the young by example that character is more valuable than anything money can ever purchase. Also, teach them that true friends won't cloak them in their wrong but will encourage them to do what is right.

Adults need to demonstrate positive family values to the young, good work ethics and the value of community. We need to pray together, love together, struggle together and stay together through hard times as well as good times. Grown folks need to go back to good parenting and stop allowing children to parent grown ups.

Our children have so called friends who dare question good parents' decisions concerning their children. Many themselves don't have parents present or have ones that neglect them. Then some young adults run to these types because they agree with *their mess. It's foolishness, because these are acquaintances that won't last, but God and family will. We love you and are not seeking to stroke your ego. We are here to direct you in the right way, that your life is prosperous.*

Do you even remember when we were a people of honor and strength? Furthermore, I ask, are you capable of teaching your children good family values, even if you and they grew up in dysfunction? If your answer is no, it is not too late. Read our rich history, view programming that is informative and associate with people who are peace lovers and not gossipmongers, no matter the skin color or economic imbalance.

Sit your children down and watch "The Great Debaters," "Malcolm X" and pictures such as "In the Pursuit of Happiness." Pull up a seat and watch stories of the life of Dr. Martin L. King, Jr., Mrs. Rosa Parks and "Hotel Rawanda."

Flood your homes with positive music, books that speak wisdom to them and people that will encourage their spiritual growth. Do for them what was done for generations of old; ones who knew what true family values were and lived by them. I encourage all to connect with those trying to improve the quality of life; not just their life, but that of humanity. I speak of people who understand that life isn't just about them, but that we are here to serve God's purpose and not our own. We are servants one of the other.

Our houses can be turned into homes, our men to fathers, women to mothers and our children to respectful young people. How you may ask? If we as a nation of people voluntarily humble ourselves under the mighty hands of God, pray fervently while seeking his face and turn from our sinful ways, God will restore us to our places of honor.

Race relations can get better if we stop being timid and all face our prejudices and bigotry. We cannot teach tolerance of others, if we are intolerant. More times than not, we associate with people who resemble us in race, beliefs, worship, likes and dislikes. This is not good enough, since it is easy to love those who are more like us, but the test and value come in loving those that are not lovable or loving.

Race relations can be improved upon too. Restoration and reconciliation is possible, but only if we unite as a people and work for it. Many of us have forgotten our strength as a people. We forget that we are better and stronger when we join together and not when we allow differences to separate us.

I am better because of you and even in-spite of you. Being with you is more important to me than being without you. After all, every fiber of who I am has your DNA written all over them. Am I conflicted? Are you really asking me that stupid question? What did you miss in reading this book, if you don't see my inner and outer conflicts. Nevertheless, I think you worthy to keep trying.

I say to my sisters and brothers, that where I offend you in this book and I am wrong, I apologize, but if the truth offends you, then you need to grow up and be honest with yourselves. After all, it is said, that the biggest fools in the world, are the ones that fool themselves.

We need to hold open the eyes of the uninformed, thereby forcing them to view the slain children from Africa to Alabama. Show them how real men and women stood and yet stand against *wrong doing. Teach them through example how to be strong, decent and compassionate people.*

Tell them of a royal people that went so wrong, but can once again become strong.

I believe in you, but it mean little if you don't believe in yourselves. These are perilous days. It is time to put foolishness to rest and get serious about yourselves. Do it now or our future as a people will be limited to prisons and graveyards. Again I ask, "What Have We Become Royal People" and what did our ancestors suffer, bleed and die for?

THE SKIN I'M IN

The skin that I am in was not of my choosing. My skin color and related characteristics are a combination of my African, Indian and American Caucasian clans.

The vessel that I came through was not of my choosing or the individual that fathered her or me. For the vessel that carried me did not determine the skin that she was in. Her Indian American mother was only 12 years of age when she was brutally raped by an adult Caucasian and left on a Pullman train heading North.

The place that I was born in was not of my choosing either. My having one drop of Negro blood meant that I was considered less than 1/8th of a human being. It was a time when the Ku Klux Klan reigned and people of color were referred to as many today are yet called, niggers.

Divination determined the skin that I am in. Forethought was in full affect when a vessel was being chosen for my carriage. Times between times were chosen for my birth, that I might witness the unusual in what the world thought was a usual place.

The South was chosen to help me develop strength through adversity and moral character through instruction that God's will prevail. It gave me an understanding that not all people of any clan are bad or good, but have choice in their actions.

We have many Caucasians who are incensed against hate mongers and are tired of being associated with their forefathers past. They stand up and verbalize their displeasure with actions that attempt to keep hate alive. Many want peace and an opportunity to live with and disagree with a person of color without it becoming racial in nature.

Stop acting like you don't see White people standing with us against racism. Stop giving credence to those who whisper, hurl or scream derogatory words at you. After all you should have learned by now, that it is not what you are called that determines who you are, but how you refer to yourselves and what you answer to.

Nothing is wrong with the word Nigger, the problem is in what it was formed for and the meaning that was given it. Further, the skin color of the user matters not. None of us should use it when addressing others. You would think the word nigger was some delicacy as much as it is used and by people of color also.

When I hear, "What's up my nigger, you be my nigger or you're my nigger," I start looking around in an attempt to see who they are talking to. You see, I know the person is not addressing me, but I get that surprised look on my face to bring to their attention that I don't like what they said.

Don't they know that the word nigger applies to anyone with a nasty disposition and that calling someone that name makes them the nigger?

Know that it is not what others call you that matters, but what you answer to and call yourselves. We allow ourselves to be named and defined by others. I say, stop answering to names that don't apply to you, and stop wearing shoes that don't fit you.

We have so much repair work to do both within and outside of our borders. Some of this damage was manufactured by outside enemies while much more was home grown.

I believe that the more we interact with one another, the more we will see that we are more alike than our differences may lead many to believe.

While we look to the right, the left is constantly faking right then moving left to keep us off balance. Also, we must stop pitting lighter skinned minorities against darker skinned minorities, in an attempt to make them feel they are better than their dark skinned relatives. The truth is that we are a blended people, even if some people don't know it or refuse to acknowledge this fact. There is no excuse for division amongst the "races," especially those of color.

Any attempt to gain status at the expense of another or become "honorary Caucasians" will in the end work against you.

We all should be as proud of our mixed heritage as we are our language. After all, within every culture, there is a subculture of people whose mannerisms cause members of their culture to be ashamed of being associated with them. If we can only accept the good things about people, we become phony. After all, none of us are perfect and the perfect one was crucified by the self-righteous.

It is up to individuals to stop associating all of a race by the actions of some in that clan.

Why does human nature lead people to quickly point out the negatives of a race and not the positive successes? What is it about skin color that so frightens us? Like it or not, at the end of the day, we all are family. If you haven't noticed it yet, our children are ahead of us. They keep trying to teach us this by crossing color, economic, cultural and religious divides to embrace each other in loving relationships.

When will the old heads learn that times are changing for the better and that they can either join the human race or be swallowed up by it?

While the skin that I am in cover blood, arteries, veins, various muscles and tendons, it also serves to help cover a heart that is filled with love and pain. Out of the skin that I am in, grows glory as a covering for my brain's command center. My skin's coloration is rich like whirled mocha, smooth like babies behinds and varying in pigmentation like grains of sand from heaven's beaches. It is resilient, classy and causes hearts to flutter upon viewing it. Sexy chocolate they say. Gorgeous skin I hear.

Much of what I do while I am in this skin can be controlled by me and much of the control will be taken away from me. My actions and reactions to all events, rather pleasant or unpleasant, will be held against me or will serve to strengthen me. Even my inactions will have an impact upon the skin that I am in.

My choosing to love and not hate, give or receive, fall or rise, will not remove me from the skin that I am in. Why then not love the skin that I am in, instead of worrying about public views of my skin? Be it dark as midnight or light as cream, I will not bleach it, use pigmentation altering methods or tanning lotions to change it.

Take a note from babies who are touched by the heart of a person as they see through God's eyes, and not their skin color. Furthermore, take a look at the children around you and see that their skin color is neither pale nor black, but shades of brown. You can't stop it. Love.....covers "a multitude of faults."

When the aging process cause the skin that I am in to wrinkle and begin to crumble, I will yet celebrate it. In that day when the decaying process takes over, as the breath of God withdraws itself, I want it to be said, that my skin served me well.

IN THE HOME

Watch what you do at home for it will spill over into your everyday life. If you are disrespectful in the home, you will likely do the same in public.

The inabilities of some people to problem solve in an effective manner, often lead them to use verbal abuse and physical violence when being confronted and confronting others. Learning tolerance of others and their beliefs can eliminate much strife. After all, people have the right to disagree, form their own opinions and without reprisals.

Since your surroundings will affect you deeply, don't allow others to push you to do wrong. Trouble may be easy to get into but I can assure you that it is difficult to get out of.

Stop going along to get along with so called friends. Get away from people who themselves do wrong and those that attempt to persuade you to follow their bad behavior.

Don't just walk young people, get in a hurry and run! Don't worry about who is looking at you or who they tell that you ran. Put a move on it and get away from those that would lead you wrong.

Make haste that you not perish.

ISSUES ATTITUDES AND PERCEPTIONS

Wherever you go and whomever you listen to, you will find that there are issues, attitudes and perceptions involved. Perceptions of people and things can create issues and attitudes. Looks, positions, thoughts, words and even silence are perceptions that create issues surrounding life.

Issues can create attitudes and attitudes can cover pain that issues cause to arise. While some people have problems with how others look, live or sound, many fail to make positive changes, because they cannot understand the true root of their problems.

Choices of partners, positions of employment or the order in which we are allowed entrance to some event, all are determined by someone's perception of us. Their attitude and issues on our manner of dress, vehicle driven, color of skin and even brand of perfume worn, determines how we are viewed. Even butt size, lip and hip size all play a part in how we are received.

Your skin is not light enough to be white or dark enough to be considered a real sister or brother. Your lips are too small and hips too flat, something else must be in you. Your butt and lips are too big to just be....you know what I mean. You own what type of car? I am sorry but I cannot be seen with you. You see, I own my own corporation, earn six figures consulting and you do what for a living? Oh, you work for some financial institution. Don't worry; someday you will meet someone that you are more compatible with.

While everyone has at least one issue with someone they either know personally, by word of mouth or have just seen them, many take issue with others based on the expectations and perceptions of others. These attitudes if left unchecked can keep us separated and captured in self-made prisons.

Be careful of how you view others, knowing that the individual spewing evil may envy the person they are attempting to discredit.

While they have an outward appearance of sleekness and knowledge, it is all rooted in deceit and lies. If you investigate their life, often you will find that they are only a shadow of their proclamations. They look and act the part that they will never get, therefore they envy those that do and can.

Watch yourself or you may miss God's greatest gift. For often God does not come the way that we expect him to come or send the individual that we thought he should send. His ways are high above ours and only the discerning heart can feel what the blinded eye cannot see.

Remember this also, that the stone the builders rejected was the "Chief Corner Stone."

PEOPLE AND ISSUES

Everyone has at least one issue with something or someone. While some are valid and very important others are frivolous and stem from envy.

Examining our issues to see where they originate is very important. In doing so we may find that our issues with people are based on differences our friends have with others.

Too often unaware people jump on the band wagon with unscrupulous people who take issue with people and things that don't concern them. Many are themselves troublemakers and when caught, make false accusations against those that see them for what they really are. Then you have those who are angry because they have failed to achieve their own goals. They are miserable and want everyone around them to be miserable.

With all that is going on in our communities, the world and in our homes, I believe that we have enough issues of our own to deal with. Why not allow those who have issues with others to handle their own problems? Why are you so involved anyway, that you allow another to lead you to mistreat someone because they have an issue with them? What is wrong with you, that you can't think for yourself? Leave them to handle their problems. As is said, "Misery loves company."

I take issue with people who degrade one another, especially women who put down other women. More often than not, these types fail to see their inadequacies and are envious of other women.

Usually when I hear women talking about other women, I tell them that it is not nice for women to put other women down. Most of the times they just cast an eye of scorn at me and continue as others join in. You see, when I speak, I have already decided that I can handle the repercussions.

They use words like, "She thinks she's cute" and "She ain't nobody." "Look at her hair, how she looks in that dress and how fat she is." You know the kind of people I am talking about, the ones that have a problem with what you do, how you do it and even who you befriend. They even take issue with how you spend your hard earned money and what your spouse purchases you.

Then you have a group of women who take issue with how you speak. They say that you sound ghetto or white. They say that you need to stop putting perm in your hair; trying to be white. Lose some weight if you want a man or gain some weight you are not white. Why are you so light? You used to be darker. Are you using bleaching cream? She thinks she is white with her black self. He thinks he is black with his light self.

Why did you give her that? She thinks she has so much. How can he purchase her that? Look at the old car he is driving. You need to buy yourself a suit.

We all have issues people. Don't allow other peoples' issues to create problems for you. Also, I say this to you, "if all of us took the first six months of each year to mind our business and the other six months of the year to leave other peoples alone, we would have a whole year to deal with our issues."

NICE

Nice is nice as long as you don't complain or become upset when taunted. You are nice as long as you don't speak out for yourself, ask questions but do as you are ordered. You are nice when you suffer in silence and allow others to take advantage of you. Nice in-spite of how you feel, just keep rolling with the punches.

Nice is as nice does and that's the way they like you. Otherwise it will be uttered, that it was nice to know you and there is the door.

Most employers are N- not

                           I-interested in the

                           C-complaints of their

                           E-employees.

What is nice about being nice if it causes you to suffer while others gain?

MEEKNESS OR WEAKNESS

Often people think others are weak because they are meek. The truth is that only the meek will in the end inhabit the Earth. Don't be fooled by meekness, because therein abides strength.

Meekness is also a control factor that many cannot understand. It helps God's children hold their tongues, bide their time and keep themselves in line.

Soon the door will swing open and the meek will walk through, then you will realize that meekness is not weakness.

DOMINATION

D – Dumb art thou
O – oh
M – man who
I – insist that he
N – now rule
A – another.
T – These think
I – in terms
O – of ownership,
N – not believing in equality.

Dominators are unhappy people that need to control others. Most only feel important when they boss others around.

If you feel like a loser and they are always the winner, you may have become the victim of a domineering person.

PANDEMONIUM

We have and are being maimed by those seeking pleasure at our expense. We are killed for sport and used as guinea pigs by those that hate Blacks, Asians, women or homosexuals in general. We are severely abused by fathers, father figures, brothers, uncles, clergy members, law enforcement personnel and all manner of caregivers. We are brutalized and told to accept it, beat and told that it is a man's right, mutilated that we may enjoy no sexual pleasure and destroyed that we may remain second class citizens.

Through lack of financial support prostitution expands to our young. Drugs help numb the pain from a legal system that fails us. Destruction rides our way and the pains of this life assail us. We watch as from another's space as they carefully place nails in our coffins, then we scream silently. A sweet song arise in our throats, it is that prayer and praise for death.

Now let us pause and pray for the godly men who remain. Let us ask the father to guide them that no harm shall come our way at their hands.

From the hands that are stretching towards us we will fear no evil, for God is with us. When we die and rest in our graves, may women have learned that our true place is in God's hands. He is our protector and captain of our souls.

Let us ask the father to continue to guide us that our end will not come soon. For in the glistening darkness, I yet see that evil hand. It stretches and strains towards us, but God has us in his hands.

Call it pandemonium, mayhem or simply chaos, I say let calm, peace and order overtake your minds, that love and not savagery reign.

INVESTING IN THE FUTURE

When you speak of investing, you speak of putting something in that you may gain. Usually it is money in an attempt to make a profit. Sacrifices in the form of time and effort is also invested, to insure a bumper crop comes from that investment. Nothing in nothing out, little in, little out for you receive according to what you invest.

On the job, are your investments only in things which will fade or are you also investing in the people you hire? In case no one sounded the alert, lower wages make for an unhappy people. Then you say, if you don't like it your replacement is standing in the wing. I say and so is yours.

Education is the key to a better future most lawmakers say. Then why is educational funding being cut and funds for weapons of true mass destruction being increased? Why are more prisons being built than educational halls for our youth? Why are tax breaks for the rich made, when the money should go to funding healthcare, higher education and job self-help programs?

Equipment seems to mean more than people, but equipment will break down without the human touch. Buildings although strong, will decay without the human touch and the best set up will fail in time, unless the human touch is administered.

Buildings are being built without the human aspect in mind. Thousands, millions and billions are paid for the physical plant, yet the human beings that make it function receive only pennies on the dollar. What is that all about?

Billions have been spent on a war that was not ours and Billions more are being spent to rebuild where we no longer belong. Where is the Billions of dollars that went through Iraq? You know what I mean. I am speaking of the funds that took a roundtrip flight back to America. Whose bank accounts are bulging with our money and who is yet benefiting from this war?

Why are soldiers' families here in America eating off food stamps and at the hands of "Feed the Children," while their loved ones bleed and die far away from home? Do you think that President Bush's family, his Cabinet members' families or any who voted for this war eats off food stamps and from "Feed the Children?" Then Senator McCain the Republican Presidential Candidate is alleged to have endorsed another 100 years in Iraq if he feels it necessary.

Who is investing in our future and that of our children, while our money is being invested in Iraq's future? Don't you know that no taxpaying citizen in America should ever lose their home, after having our tax dollars given and thrown away?

Fall on hard luck, get sick and need public assistance and see what will happen to you and your family, especially if you own any property. You will be forced to pay it back as a lean will be placed on your property. Even if you die, your family will have to repay what you have paid for through your tax dollars. Who is going to pay back the American people all the money that has been taken from them and misused by the government and big businesses? Who is going to give us amnesty and forgive our debt within the USA?

We have no recourse. Yet we keep electing lawmakers that are themselves lawbreakers and interested in their own well being only.

In reading the book of Genesis, we learned that Cain killed Able. When will we learn that a nation divided against itself is headed for a fall and a hungry people will get tired and some day turn and eat on you? Believe me when I say, that what was done in the dark, God in his justice will reveal to the world.

BBC World News America please don't bow down. Set the record straight and tell the American people the truth. We hunger for truth and are repulsed by the lies that are being told.

RIDING WITH DRUNKS ON
THE ROAD TO DESTRUCTION

When there was prayer in schools, there was respect, concern and a conduct of honor. Teamwork existed amongst parents, teachers and students. The golden rule was in force for children and adults displayed morality.

Today we often hear educators say, "It's my way or the highway" or "I've got mine, you can get yours the best way that you can." What a horrible thing to hear an educator say to students.

Many of our children are riding on the road to destruction with those drunk in mind and spirit. While money, sex and positions are first on many minds, years ago dedication and making a difference in some child's life was the driving force for school administrators.

What can we do when parents, the clergy, educators and the government who is in control of our tax dollars are abandoning our children? What can we do when our tax dollars keep increasing and our children's educational level keep declining?

Have you seriously wondered why many educational systems of today cannot perform at the educational levels of the 1960's, seeing they have greater resources today? Seriously I ask, "What is missing today that yesteryears had?" Few seem to believe that parents, teachers and administrators dedication to educating students is what is lacking. Added to this is what drugs have done to our children through parents that were addicted while carrying them. Then you have chemical products including medications in our food and drinking water.

Did you ever consider if the water was being treated for all the drugs that go out in urine, feces and that are being poured down toilets? Then you wonder what is wrong with our children and adults.

Have we allowed God and family to be separated by laws formed in an attempt to give "everyone" rights? In the name of freedoms, have we given it where it does not belong? Have we over medicated our children and adults?

I say that now is the time for the American people to come together and demand what is ours. We have been given an opportunity to shine or further descend into the abyss of division.

If we fail this time, we have ourselves to blame. Choose wisely people, because the world is watching us. Eight years of hell will be nothing compared to what is to come, if we repeat past mistakes.

Choose wisely America; having been given another opportunity for TRUE CHANGE. History is waiting and it will be recorded for future generations to see our wisdom or foolishness. Our children are watching too.

It is now or never. The sleeping giant called the American people have been awakened. Then let us be honest with ourselves and admit that our past actions and former inactions is the cause of this generations moral and economic decline. Furthermore, if we fail to get it right this 2008 General Election, future generations will curse our names.

Years ago parents worked hard too. Some worked two jobs and had little money, but they were there for their children. Many people studied by kerosene lamps and the light of fireplaces. They walked to school, sometimes with shoes whose soles were of cardboard. Many wore coveralls or handmade dresses. Today providing things for children is the flavor of the day and at the expense of love and time given. Television, video games and MySpace.com has replaced family gatherings.

Years ago even teachers stayed after school to help students, because they were concerned and not because they were forced to do it. Slower students were placed between two fast students to help them learn. We used the buddy system.

Teachers, during the 1950–1960's did not become annoyed when students asked questions. They wanted them to participate; to learn and dream.

Our children face too many problems today. They are pressured from all sides and lack the tools to cope. Young people are expected to act like adults, make adult decisions and face adult prejudgments. The odd thing is that often adults act like children and provide negative tools to young people when dealing with unpleasant issues.

We must be consistent with our teaching, living and our actions. When we do wrong, we must allow our young to see us apologize and harshly condemn our own bad actions.

People as a whole are out of control. We live in an all about me society. Things have become more important than human beings.

Life is more than expensive shoes, clothing, vehicles, fingernails, stocks, bonds and weaves. It is more critical than sex, second homes, vacations and positions of power. It should be about God and family, since in the end we will be answerable for our actions.

I say that we all can make it to the top of the hill, if we give each other a hand up, not out. We need to learn that everyone has something to offer if only priceless words of wisdom.

Those that are drinking, smoking and having sex with the young need to stop corrupting them. You are their teachers, parents, preachers and lawmakers. Stop drugging them with things, promises and lies. Let them keep their innocence for they will grow up soon enough. It is time to go back to the basics before psychiatric wards, prisons and coffins consume most of our children.

We as adults have fallen down on our jobs and have failed our children. Further, we have allowed unscrupulous educators and lawmakers who are themselves lawbreakers to team up with their legal eagle partners and pass laws and implement statutes that place our families in harms way.

Now we find it very difficult to strip them of the powers we freely bestowed upon them. We must learn from our mistakes that we not repeat them. We must acknowledge that we have put unscrupulous people in charge of our lives then seek to remedy the situation. We need to read closely the laws that our legislative bodies are approving, for many are to our detriment.

We as a united people need to return to the value systems of old; not prejudices of old. When we elevate others, we too will be enlarged.

Knowledge is power and what you don't know can kill you. All of us will either pay now or later to better our tomorrows. I say that now is better than later, for the longer we take the more destruction is being done.

Will we get books today and functional educational systems or a bullet and penal institution tomorrow? Which will it be?

I went to school in the segregated South. It was a place of fear of White folks, if you got out of what they called "your place." It was Montgomery, Alabama to be exact; the State that George

Wallace governed and the KKK ruled. Yet with love, concern and dedication of parents, educators and the clergy we survived to become a great people.

Today, in great numbers, our children are on the road to destruction and the culprits are often parents, teachers, administrators and even the clergy. It is time to awaken community and demand a quality education for our children and grandchildren. Adopt a school and share your knowledge with the young. After all, this country was built on our backs. There is no time to retire or rest. We must work while it is daytime for after the grave we all can rest.

Come on grandma, put on your shields of faith, roll up your stockings, put on your Sunday hat and grab that old cane. You too grandpas, buckle up your suspenders, throw down the tobacco and snuff can and put your teeth back in. Why you ask? You are not dead yet, it is time to go to battle for your children's children and kids of your communities.

It's time to take back the schools that your hard earned money is paying for. No longer allow them to lock and block you out of what the community is paying for. In like manner, we must stop esteeming those in the soul saving business that sells our souls for name recognition and power. Remember that relationships, positions and interest come and go, but what we do in Jesus name will stand in the end.

Come on America, can't you see that our children are riding with drunks on the road to destruction? What are you going to do to save our children?

A JOKE THAT ENDED IN WAR

What started as a joke six years ago has now ended in war. It started in 1993 between the East and West sides of Uniondale, New York. East against West, our children are now left to die, because what started as a joke has now ended in war.

Like hoodlums they ran and banged loudly upon the N45 bus. I thought they were trying to simply get on the bus. As they boarded one paid while the rest dashed down the isle, all the time spewing vile words. Each had entered to attack two young men that sat in the back. It was eight on two as more boarded through the back door. They disrespected the driver, riders and women alike. Even the lady sitting with the young men were disrespected. I leapt to my feet and said, "Sit down or get off the bus!"

They continued using foul language fiercely as they spit on their victims. They challenged them to do battle as onlookers said and did nothing.

Again, I demanded, "Sit down or get off this bus!" As they exited, I turned to those under attack and urged the young men not to go back. One was bent on revenge and said, "They spit in my face and on my clothing!" I said, "Son spit will dry but too many may die if you go back instead of leaving it alone."

As the bus stopped, the victims ran to get reinforcements to go to battle. All I could do was pray that God keep them from themselves.

To my surprise a man in his twenties replied, "This started six years ago when I was in their high school. We started it as a joke. I never thought that it would lead to this. I thought it was over."

Special Note: Be careful oh ye people of the legacy that you leave behind. Wherever you leave your footsteps a blessing or curse will remain. In this case, what started as a joke in 1993 had escalated into a war in 1999.

DIARRHEA OF THE MOUTH

Most of us have met people who cause discord everywhere they go. I am speaking of persons that interject their two cents worth where they don't belong. Then they run up and down, back and forth just spewing nothings in an attempt to be recognized. Well I am here to say that they have "Diarrhea of the Mouth." I speak of people "flapping those rubber lips" as my sister Izora Robinson often say; loose bowels that flow out with no control; fool lips with slime running out; picking at the skills of others in an attempt to emulate them and steal their thunder. If this is you, baby....you are suffering from terminal "Diarrhea of the Mouth."

There she goes again; head bobbing like a bobble doll, as she run to spread lies to the unwise. She has "Diarrhea of the Mouth," loose bowels that even she is incapable of shutting down. Running about whispering lies to the unwise and turning fools against the wise in an attempt to be recognized. These types are the worst of enemies and often wonder why others look at them strange and don't want to be in their company.

In case you never heard, loose lips are even capable of "sinking battle ships," starting wars, ruining marriages and relationships. Loose lips cause lives to be altered in lies and truths. A loose lip person cannot be trusted because they can't keep a confidence.

So you thought that you were immune to those with "Diarrhea of the Mouth?" Baby you had better think again! The joke is already on you. While you looked at me as the culprit, with the slight of hand and blink of the eye, your "friend" is the one who revealed your most private secrets. The joke is on you baby for I know more than you think. Take care and remember that what goes around truly comes back around.

I say, stop running to and fro with half-truths; telling lies about others and even your accomplishments. Stop being so eager to lead and learn how to follow. Don't run with every little thing you hear, everything you thought was said and even make up lies in an attempt to gain what someone else has. You don't know what it cost them to be where they are and who they are.

Fool, you are not cool. You are an imitator, thief and unbalanced person.

Then there are those that even imitate the dead. Lacking confidence in themselves, they attempt to move like, dress like and even sing like the dead.

Special Notes: If you become the person that you were designed to be, the world will be propelled forward as your uniqueness shine through.

Keep in mind also, that advances come through inventiveness and not replications. Don't lose yourself in others by becoming a cheap copy. Strive to be a great original.

DEFINING OURSELVES
BEYOND TITLES

Today is our day; the day to give ourselves the freedom to explore and embrace who we really are, beyond our birth names, nicknames and married names. Outside of how friends describe us, how co-workers view us, the fronts put forth in lies and even what enemies call us, who are we?

How do we the people define ourselves beyond the titles of our educational achievements, job titles and the badges worn? Who are we really beyond our titles; when we are alone and no one is looking at us? What lurk in our hearts regarding others when we pass them in hallways, reach out to dress their wounds or when we are confronted by those we feel superior to?

The way we define ourselves beyond our titles are important, but more than our definition of ourselves is the how we interact with others. Our actions, inactions and reactions speak louder than words ever could.

While titles are necessary measures of identification and are helpful in maintaining order, they do not signify that one person is better than another. However, they are markers that tell people something about your capabilities, positions and calling. Titles also serve to direct us as in names on buildings, streets and airplanes.

Often people who are defined by titles began to huff, puff and quote their credentials when they fail to get their way. Many are abrupt with those they feel to be beneath them and demand special treatment. Their associations usually are only with those they feel are of little threat to them.

Personally, I need people around me that will challenge me to grow. They need to be confident, honest and spiritual. Negative people will drain you and eventually betray your trust.

Ask yourself, do I interact with people based on their status and or level of importance? Perhaps you make eye contact with, smile at or speak to people based on their shoe brand, dress type or vehicle driven? Does hairstyle, skin color, faith practiced or nationality determine who you associate with? Is it all about what you can gain or are you cordial to everyone?

I say to you that knowingly or unknowingly our actions and or inactions will define us far above the titles worn. Further, our interactions will either bring us together or separate us.

Bear in mind, that there are no sensitivity programs or fancy slogans that will change those who are not willing to change. Sensitivity comes from within and the lack thereof is a character flaw.

Only when the "M" in the word me is turned upside down, do we get the word "WE." All of us need to understand that we are spending our lives together. Like it or not, most of our waking hours are spent with the people that we work with. Together we can get the job done, but not if we allow ourselves to be separated by titles, feelings of inadequacy and those that love discord.

Remember that you are important simply because you were born. Also keep in mind that the greatest of all was a servant. His name is Jesus the Christ.

ENOUGH I SAY

Often I hear people complaining about how bad this world and life is. Most fail to understand that it is not our world or life, but people that create problems.

From the creation of the Heavens, Earth and its inhabitants, "God saw everything that he had made, and behold it was very good." Genesis 1:31 the KJV The Holy Bible.

As it was then so it is now. Nothing changed in the Garden of Eden except Eve, when of her own volition she was enticed, drawn away and did eat "of the tree of the knowledge of good and evil." Genesis 2:17. However when Adam did likewise and disobeyed a direct commandment from God, who in verse 16 of Genesis 2 said, "And the Lord God commanded the man, saying, of every tree of the garden thou mayes freely eat: but of the tree of the knowledge of good and evil, thou shalt not eat of it: for in the day that thou eatest thereof thou shalt surely die," the door of sin and death for all of humanity was opened. Then the blame game started when God questioned Adam on who told him that he was naked. He blamed Eve and Eve blamed the serpent. Neither of them took responsibility for their own actions, but chose to blame another.

I believe that God would have given Adam another woman if he had obeyed God and not eaten of the fruit himself. After all God gave the man dominion over the Garden and the woman.

Today I see the same thing happening. People blaming the world and even God for their predicament. If the truth be told, people are the number one problem and not the world that God created.

The world was made perfect. Humankind blocks the progress and peace of others. They are the ones who set up roadblocks, injure, kill and maim.

It is their bad choices, associations and decisions that have altered the structure of humanity, the air we breathe and the very core of our faith. They are the liars that have twisted the truth and deceived fools into following their stinking way of thinking.

I say enough with bad asses, liars, cheats and the likes. Enough regarding the lies about weapons of mass destruction and how the billions of dollars are being spent in Iraq and Afghanistan. Enough of the high cost of oil and the lies given for high surcharges by power authorities. Enough of lawmakers who are themselves lawbreakers. They misuse the legal system and without repercussions. Enough of corrupt politicians who lie to get elected then fail to look out for the best interest of the people. Enough of lying preachers who use the pulpit for personal gain and family expansion. Enough of my wasting time on things that cannot be changed and wishing I could start over again.

Enough I say, enough!

RUSHING LIFE AWAY

Today too many people are in a hurry and for just about everything. They disregard the rights of others and think nothing of it. Many fail to stop at stop signs, red lights and even to yield the right of way. Some kill pedestrians and continue on their way. Don't they realize that they are rushing their lives away?

Often these types sit and blow their horns fiercely at those of us who stop at stop signs, red lights and don't drive off as soon as lights change. They flip their middle finger at those who refuse to speed as they drive on their bumpers and some even resort to road rage. Don't they know that they are rushing their lives away?

We all need to stop and smell sweet flowers, listen to birds chirping and the voice of God. Take time for our children, listen to what they are saying, pay attention to their actions and train them in the way they should go. Kiss your spouse, help some senior cross the street or just stop and say a prayer.

Slow down and change your today that you may have better tomorrows. Slow down and live before life pass you bye. Slow down people and glimpse God in others, maybe then you can see him in yourselves. Slow down I say and stop "Rushing Life Away."

EXCEPTIONAL ME

No, I am not the exception to the rule. I am not a different kind of NEGRO, BLACK, AFRICAN or MINORITY because of my intelligence or mixed heritage. I am in the majority and this you would see if you removed the blinders of discrimination from your eyes.

I am not the exception to the rule. What rule and who made up this rule anyway?

Limits that are placed on people and spaces often hinder them from pursuing their dreams. As does a lack of opportunity and dislike of the shell that it comes from.

"Exceptional Me?" If I am to be known for something, let it not be for being exceptional. Please say that I was not afraid to face the real me. Tell them that I have embraced her and delivered her to the world.

However, if I am to be labeled exceptional, let it be because the I AM said that I am.

WAITING IN ANTICIPATION

Most of my life, I have waited in anticipation for something. At the top of the list was deliverance from abuse and waiting for love.

I tried to form friendships where they did not exist, only to find that I had confided in wolves dressed in sheep's clothing. What did I expect would happen, when I tried to walk in places my feet should never have trod?

Bound as a child to the abuses of family and the segregated South, it became difficult to recognize love and true friendships. Then abuse as a wife by the male who promised to love, honor and cherish me, further caused my ability to discern good people from bad to be skewed.

Seeking relief from lawmakers and churches were of little help, since many enforcers and clergy were themselves corrupt. Then my turning to co-workers became a worse mistake, since envy and jealousy lead to more distress. Why did I seek their help and what did I hope to gain anyway, as I sat "Waiting In Anticipation" of freedom for myself?

Tested that I may have testimonies and dwell where eagles soar, I had to learn to stop waiting for what I could do for myself. As one door closed another one swung wide open, that I no longer sit "Waiting in Anticipation" for what I can do for myself.

I learned that life is more than relationships between men and women. Some people will never fit in with society, since they are destined to walk with God. Now I sit "Waiting in Anticipation" only of the promises of God.

GOING THROUGH MOTIONS

I have been going through motions of living while dying inside, feigning happiness on the outside while crying inside. I motioned to others that everything was all right, but I was really going through the motions of life.

You see, going through motions became my means of survival. Now that the mask is off I can start a new life. I had to learn that without pain sometimes there is no gain and that sorrow can bring about the appreciation of joy and give new hope on tomorrow.

From now on I will stop going through motions and just be me. You see, it is a waste of time to go through motions that keep you from being free. You will never come into your own going through motions. Release you, that life may flow and the real you may show. Come forward and care not if they like or accept you. Just stop going through motions and be free.

PAIN AND PROMISES

What do you do when the pain before you seem greater than the promises made to you? Do you go forward to victory or stop in anticipation of failure?

It is not always easy to collect on the promises of God, especially if we fail to do the "if." While he promised the this and that, we often forget that we are in control of the release switch. Our healing and receiving is all based on "if" we ask for the "it" in faith, "if" we seek the "it" diligently and "if" we believe with nothing wavering.

When we fail to do our part, remember that the failing is not in God but us. He will always deliver that which he promised and not withhold any good thing from his children.

BOUND BUT NOT GAGGED

Most of my life I have been bound by something. There were even times when I was gagged as well. I have been bound to the ideas and ideals of others and demanded to be loyal where no loyalty was given. I have been ordered not to reveal the indiscretions of others and ordered to do wrong on behalf of manipulators. Bound by marriage vows, contracts, promises and even oaths of office. Religiosity tried to rope me but Christianity saved me, that I may be bound to the laws and will of God.

I can tell it all wherever I go and to whomever will listen, that a fall is on the way and I am in the middle. Ordered to be silent for I know too much and silence demanded in exchange for being left alone. Bound but not gagged I loudly exclaim that the fear of God and not mankind is where true wisdom began.

Know that there is an enemy within that works with the ones without. Often it looks like us but nonetheless is an enemy. Do not be fooled and do not fail to watch and pray or you too may find yourself bound and gagged by listening to fools instead of thinking for yourselves.

LETHAL IS THE WEAPON

Housed within the mouth is a most lethal weapon. This weapon is more lethal than guns, knives and bombs. When it rears its ugly head all run for cover, because it can drop the best of mankind.

The tongue is a fire, a small world filled with iniquity. It is so lethal that its victims seldom recover, from this lethal weapon covered by a smile.

People, words kill and go deeper than any bullet ever could. It divides asunder, parts friendships and then move on to others. Be careful of what you say or you may fall victim to that lethal weapon known as the tongue.

GOING THROUGH THE
WILDERNESS

I was brought out of Egypt but found myself wandering through life's wilderness. I became wild and wilder as life's pleasures overtook my good senses. I wandered through many mazes that were filled with twists and turns, as I walked through the wilderness and could not find my way home. My place of bondage called me saying please come back home, but I kept on wandering trying to find my true home.

Stuck in bondage for many years, I continued to walk in circles trying to find my way home. Where had I gone wrong? Oh help me dear God!

Life is a wilderness that is filled with many twist and turns. Your only means of escape is to rise above your circumstances. With wisdom as your guide, success at last will come, if you do not stop, but go through the wilderness of life.

IN MY FATHER'S EYES

In my father's eyes I am beautiful and without spot or wrinkle. He looks past the weight gain, gray hair, age spots, wrinkles and this aging body. My father knows the real me housed within this shell. He sees the beauty in my spirit and soul.

In my father's eyes I am perfected. You see that is one of the benefits of joint heir-ship. Through Jesus I am looked upon as righteous. I like being looked at through my father's eyes.

In my father's eyes, I am more than a conqueror. I am everything that my big brother is because he came, died, conquered death and arose from the dead all for me. He is my strength when I become weak and is my way back to God. All I have to do is simply say, "I'm strong." That is enough for my father to act.

In my father's eyes I am love, because my father sees me in his image. He through Jesus sees me not as I am but as I ought to be.

When all is said and done, I am glad that how I am seen in my father's eyes is what will save me in the end.

What do you think about that?

MY HERO

One day while standing in my bedroom I began to cry profusely. All of a sudden I was overwhelmed with love for God. Tears began to flow as I said, "I love you God" and "you are MY HERO." I beat upon my chest to signal that it was coming from my heart. All I could do was lift my hands in praise and exclaim how much I loved him as tears kept rolling down my face.

God is MY HERO. He has never failed or left me alone. He is my peace and hope for today and all of my tomorrows. It is he who taught me how to decrease that he may increase and lap water as I go.

I humbly bow my head in reverence to the only one that I can completely trust. He is MY HERO.

IT WILL MESS YOU UP

Fear will mess you up. It will keep you from going forward and from receiving the blessings of God. It can turn you against your brother; cause you to kill your sister and even your own mother. Fear, it will mess you up.

Some fear commitment while others fear upward mobility. Many fear standing alone and fear taking a stand. Others fear losing control and not being recognized. Fear of loving, not being loved and of skin color all will mess you up.

Why are people so fearful and why are they so angry? Don't they understand that it is fear that will mess them up?

While they worry and fear death, it is life's decisions that will mess them up. Fear can cheat you out of your life's victories and leave you down and out. It will knock you down and refuse to let you up. So remember people, never allow fear in for it will mess you up.

ACE AND ICE

Ace and ice walk hand in hand that friendships may be formed and disassociations made. Ace is a friend that can be counted on and ice will disassociate from those that prove themselves enemies.

Thin ice can easily break and those standing upon it will surely fall into distressful waters. Walk carefully and be cautious or you may find that ace has turned to ice and a friendship to a disassociation.

Often people take advantage of friendships. They think that they can do anything and yet remain a friend. True friends understand limitations and the rarity of a solid friendship.

A friend is not one who would seek to destroy you but one that would build you up. Neither would a friend place a dagger in your back then twist it for their sick pleasure. Friends don't seek to destroy others reputation, marriages or become jealous of their accomplishments. If this occurs to you, what you have is a wolf in sheep's clothing and not a friend. Cut them loose and don't fret, because they were not your friend anyway.

"Can you hear me now?" Am I getting through to you girlfriend?

ON MY KNEES I

While searching for a chart one day at work, I found myself down on my knees. I looked down and asked myself, "Why are you on your knees?" My head rolled right gently and I beheld the chart that I was seeking. Down on my knees I found what I was searching for.

Sometimes you have to kneel down to find answers to what you are searching for. If you are not willing to get down on your knees in prayer, you may not be allowed to stand on your feet.

Just like a true father, he had gotten his point across. If I could get down on my knees at work to locate a chart, I could get down on my knees and pray to him.

That night down on my knees, I prayed for answers to what I was searching for.

THE INTROVERTED
EXTROVERT

Have you ever attempted to hide from someone like my friend Catherine New? You know people like me who are somewhat reclusive or may I say a hermit of sort. Well, this is a hard task to accomplish with Catherine for a friend.

Ms. Vociferous is determined to pull you out of your Hermit state. You will hear her say something like, I see you so don't try to hide from me or get your butt out here. You see Catherine knows when you do that, you are not living but just existing. She will command you to come out of hiding.

Don't bother to exclaim to her that you have nothing to wear, you have gained weight, your eyebrows fell off or saying I cannot be seen in daylight, because it is all to no avail. Catherine will say "Come as you are darling" and you will be left asking yourself if she meant to come in your birthday suit. Further she will exclaim, "Who cares if you gained weight."

Then on your eyebrow issue, she may ask if you learned to draw in grade school. If your answer is yes, she may tell you to paint new eyebrows on and "come on over." As for my Vampire issue, she may say just use some tanning cream and you won't go up in flames.

Catherine leaves no excuses for your introverted butt not to show up. Thank God for Catherine because she forces this introvert to become extroverted even if only for a little while.

PROCRASTINATION

Procrastination is not a friend but an enemy of the mind. It delays you by saying tomorrow and later in the day. It will erode away your confidence and leave you in the dirt. It casts doubt on your future and even voids your word.

Try not to become a procrastinator, or you may find that life has passed you as a result of your procrastination. Worse than that, you have failed to complete your tasks and it is now time to die.

NOW AND RIGHT NOW

Now, tomorrow, next week or later, whatever the call it will always come down to right now. Now is the time of your deliverance and tomorrow another battle to win. Next week come what may and later in a day may never come your way.

Right now has called. Your healing and blessings all knock at your door. Front and center they say, for now and right now is your time oh child of mine.

I WONDERED WHAT WAS
WRONG WITH ME

My body, my spirit and my soul are not one. When I would do good evil attempts to prevent me. My soul is caught in the middle looking side to side, back and forth all in an attempt to see which will win. More often than not my soul wins. Yet there are times when my flesh talks to my mind and they compromise. With a massage in tow and no man to know, then I wondered what was wrong with me oh soul of mine.

A war is going on and my soul is in the line of fire. The body of sin is fighting for control in a battle that it cannot win. So when I wonder what is wrong with me, I have to keep in mind, that it is my three people warring in an attempt to gain control.

Special Note: When an opponent has pinned you down like a wrestler his opponent, always remember that God is waiting for you to reach out to him. Just reach out and tag God, because he cannot be defeated.

He is waiting for you. What are you waiting on? Give the "it" to him!

I TAGGED GOD

When I give a fight all that I have and my strength begin to wane, I tag God. I tag him when I cannot run any faster, jump any higher or see my way clear as I am being pummeled by life's circumstances.

Don't let the referee count you out when God is standing there with outstretched hands, asking you to tag him. Don't listen to the voices in your head that say you can't win. You are not in this alone and the battle is not yours anyway, it is God's.

Reach out and tag him. Tag him when family members are acting like they have lost their minds. Tag him when co-workers are lying and scheming on you. Tag God when the doctor tells you that there is no cure for your illness. Reach out and tag him when your opponent has you on the ropes and you cannot see how to hit back through the lies, blood, sweat and tears. Go on and do it, tag God! Do it with a fierceness and assurance that "No weapon that is formed against thee shall prosper: and every tongue that shall rise against thee in judgment thou shalt condemn." Isaiah 54:17. Furthermore, Jesus told us in his word, "He that is without sin, let him cast the first stone."

After all, you were directed to say that you are strong and not be strength. Why you may ask? It is because when you obey his directive of, "Let the weak say I'm strong," it gives him permission to take over like a tag team member and kick your opponent's butt. Further it gives him permission to act on your behalf and gives you the confidence that when you call, he will show up. After all our father is omnipotent, omnipresent and omniscient. No force can defeat us, as long as he and his word remain within us.

Most people will follow the directions for baking a cake or the instructions on their medication bottles, but for some reason don't believe they need to follow God's rules for living a better life.

It is simple, if we call him, he will answer and if we cry, he has promised to say "Here I am." What's so difficult about this?

If you practice calling him when you are not in trouble, it will be easy to call him when you are. He will not disappoint you and will arrive at the right time. Go ahead and put him to the test; that is if he is your Daddy. Call Daddy, when you get in trouble.

Remember this; he will not enter the ring unless you invite him. You must reach out and tag him, because he will not break the rules.

Trouble will come your way and sometimes it is self made. However the fact that you are yet in it, says that you are not capable of extracting yourself. Tag God! I dare you to tag him when things get tough; when you have exhausted all of your means and no resolution is in sight. I double dog dare you to tag God. I did, I do and will continue to tag him. He knows how long I need to be in the fire and will extricate me in due season.

"I Tagged God!" I tagged him and he came through for me. I tagged him and he calmed the storms in my life, helped me to go through what I needed to go through and not vacation where I didn't belong.

Don't be afraid and don't be ashamed to ask for his help. After all God is waiting for us to tag him. Tag God! Take him up on his offer. Tag him that the victory may be yours. I did and he came to my rescue. "I Tagged God."

WHEN YOU AWOKE
THIS MORNING

When you awoke this morning, did it cross your mind that you have the activities of all your limbs or the movement of at least some of them? Did you realize that your mind was in order or at the least you had cognizant moments? When you awoke this morning did it even dawn on you that you are not paralyzed, crippled, blind or deft? Even if you are or have any other life altering conditions, did you realize that what seems like a curse is wrapped up in blessings? Being alive gives you an opportunity to pray one more time, tell someone that you love them or get yourself together.

When you awoke this morning, did you thank God for whatever state you are in, realizing that having life is in itself a blessing? If you did not, I challenge you to look to God and thank him for every situation.

You see, when I awoke this morning, I realized just how lucky I was to be alive. I was thankful to have God on my side and to have been born even in the segregated South. It made me proud, because I am who I am because of my life experiences. More than these, being alive give me another chance to repent of my sins, forgive those who hurt me and continue serving God in my small way.

I know that I am alive by design and not chance. The mission that must be completed is not my own but his. Ready and willing I go forward and with an assurance that life is not just about me. It is only what I do in Jesus name that will be left standing in the end.

Again I ask you, when you awoke this morning, did you bother to thank God for being or did you think that you somehow managed this feat? Did you challenge yourself to do something for someone else in Jesus' name, or is everything done in your name?

Know children, that in the morning when you arise, that it is God and not you who have caused negatives not to befall you.

BEING THANKFUL

When I awoke this morning I was thankful. I realized that it was by God's grace and mercy that I had bodily functions, health, children and grandchildren. My spouse, friends or just having me was reason enough to be thankful. Suddenly, I realized that being alive had given me another chance to change my stinking way of thinking and climb out of my pity party.

I realized that many others could not see through the clouds to see that their tomorrows will be better through God. Also I know that my thankfulness should not be based on the abundance of things, but the fact that I have been granted life.

Yes there are surgical scars, medications that help me live and physical conditions that limit me. You too may have some life altering conditions, be on oxygen, need a walker or have a wheelchair beside your bed, but you are still here.

The Iraq or Afghanistan Wars may have left you scarred from within and from without, but by the mercy of God you came home alive. Desert Storm or the Gulf conflict may have scarred you too, but someone yet loves you. It could have been the Vietnam War or life wars here in the States, yet I say use your experiences to help others and make a difference in this world.

You, yes you there in a prison of the mind or behind prison bars, you too have reason to be thankful. Having life gives you an opportunity to change, grow and gain eternal life. Even if you are separated from loved ones by being in a psychiatric ward or due to your family being scattered, I say that the fact that you are yet alive makes all the difference. The measure of health, wealth and movement that you have should be enough for you to be thankful. As should surviving Hurricanes, Tsunamis, fires, earthquakes and life's many tests.

If you have a can of beans, bread and water or only a candy bar to eat be thankful. Why, because things can be replaced, but not you. Also, there are those who have nothing including hope.

Rejoice and again I say rejoice in whatever situation you find yourself. For wherever there is life, hope remains.

WHAT'S ON YOUR MIND

The mind is the seat of information and nothing can enter the heart without first filtering through the mind. Also, little can come out of the mouth without first being a thought that was reflected on over and over again until the heart caught it.

We need to guard our thoughts that they not accept evil ideas and filter those thoughts into our hearts. If allowed, it will stick in our hearts and eventually we will speak it into existence.

Rebuking high minds, casting down imaginations and eradicating fear take's power, love and soundness of mind. Not submitting to seducing spirits takes power, love of self and a right thinking mind. All of which comes from God.

Garbage in, garbage out. Good thoughts in, good thoughts out.

WITH EYES THAT COULD NOT SEE

While standing at a bus stop one day, I finally realized that the man I should be with was the one who I always took for granted. Tears began to stream down my face in broad daylight as hindsight said; he was there all the time.

Even when I failed to listen to him and entertained the wrong man, he wiped my tears away instead of judging me. I had been so busy searching for the love of my life, that I could not see him right there in my face. I would call to tell him of each love gone wrong and he advised me, comforted me and remained my friend. Little did I know how much I had hurt him every time I ran to him when another relationship went wrong. Instead of giving him a chance, I kept giving my heart to another.

Sex was never his aim, nor using me. All he wanted was a chance to show me what a real man was. He wanted to heal my heart from within and stop bandaging it from without. Because he kept silent while continuing to comfort me, I did not realize just how much I had hurt him.

Now with a gait that is sometimes slower, hair grayer and eyesight that is challenging at times, I clearly see that God is the only one who loves me just as I am. He has always been a faithful Lord, gentle master and friend.

Presenting my body to him is not for sex, but to keep me safe from sexual predators and a commutable sexual disease. His intentions are all pure and not to earn some notch on his belt or have something to brag about to others.

It has taken me a long time, but I finally realized that what I was looking for was with me all the time.

Special Note: It takes more than sex to maintain a good relationship. I prefer God over superficial feelings that change and fade away. If sex is all you have to offer, step off, because I can live without sex but some commutable diseases kill.

PAT TURNER AND ME

Pat, turner and me are very good friends. We go everywhere together and cannot be separated. If it was not for pat and turner where would I be?

Pat keeps me on the straight and narrow, while turner takes care of the curves. Pat and turner are my strong supporters and take me to each destination. It is pat that hits the pavement as turner turns the corners. I thank God for feet to walk with from place to place.

While I am thankful that I now have a vehicle, I always want to remember when pat and turner was all we as a people had.

FOOLS MONEY

*There is an old saying, that "money and fools soon part company."
They squander their inheritance, and then turn to others expecting
them to share theirs. Pinching a little from this one and even
more from the rest, they again amass wealth. However little has
been learned as they repeat past behavior.*

*Don't lose your God given inheritance to fools; be it money or
other blessings. Hold fast to what is yours and pray for guidance
when attempting to help others.*

Don't let it be said that you too are a fool.

IT'S THE GIFT

Powerful messages are sometimes delivered through lying lips, as are words of wisdom sometimes delivered from hypocrites' hearts. How can this be; blessings and cursing coming from the same place? It's not the person but the gift.

Maybe some day if we keep praying, they will catch up with their gift(s) and then become truly awesome. In the meantime take what you can and forgive their shortcomings where you can. For a perfect person people did kill and left the wounded behind to do their best.

Remember that when you see people standing tall and speaking words of wisdom, that it may not be them, but the gift within them.

SIX LEVELS OF YOU AND ME

Just like a car's engine, our minds and bodies operate by levels. Each of these levels causes a different reaction within and without. What level are you operating on today?

At level "1," BEIGE, I am totally relaxed as I rise to ready myself for work. Stumbling to the bathroom, kitchen and my clothing, I slowly become conscious of my surroundings.

At level "2," OLIVE GREEN, I have stirred more, had my coffee or breakfast and am ready to go to work.

At level "3," BABY BLUE, I stroll in to work and my engine has reached its normal state of operation. I am calm and ready to start. What a beautiful day.

At level "4," LIME GREEN, my anxiety level begins to rise as I hear the rings of phones and the demands start. I'm all right and everything is under control.

At level "5," ORANGE RUST, my stress level is near the boiling point and I am about to lose control. I have been yelled at, lied on and had half of my behind chewed off. My mind is saying, "Somebody hold me back."

At level "6," RED, every button has been pushed, every lie has been told and like the bull I am ready to charge. Back me down now before one more thing cause me to blow my top.

———————

As we continue to work together, may our combined efforts help each member of this "TEAM" not explode like TNT.

GETTING DOWN THE BASICS

The Bible contains instructions that can assist us in navigating through this life and in achieving eternal life. They were left by and through Jesus, to help us discern his voice from that of mankind and the fallen. Following these lessons all depend on our faith and willingness to study and do.

Below I will share with you the decoding of the letters that make up the word BIBLE. While I do not know where it originated, I agree with it.

> *B –"Basic*
>
> *I – instructions*
>
> *B – before*
>
> *L – leaving*
>
> *E – Earth."*

To complete any task, we must at least have the ability to follow basic instructions. Therefore I take a closer look at these five letters.

Basic speaks to what's essential, necessary, critical and fundamental to complete tasks.

Instructions are directives, information, advice and orders given.

Before speaks to what is required beforehand, prior to and in advance of getting started.

Leaving speaks of departing, taking leave and saying goodbye.

God through Jesus so loved us that he left the Holy Spirit as a comforter, guide and reminder of his words that we have learned. He also left detailed instructions in the Bible for us to follow.

Earth is the planet; the visible world as we know it. You may believe or not believe in God, but one thing is for sure, we all know someone who has died. You can no longer see them or feel their physical bodies, but that doesn't mean their existence has ceased.

With an assurance I say to you, that there is an invisible world; a place that cannot be seen with the natural eye. It exists in-spite of your disbelief or inability to see and intuit it.

At age five, I witnessed a man that I had never seen before or since, walk through a solid wall. Yes I said it and I did not stutter. My mother, sister and I lived in a Columbus Street apartment in Montgomery, Alabama. I left our kitchen, went through our living room and placed one foot on the stairs. I no more than placed a foot on the stairs before looking up into the face of a man. He was smiling and waving at me. I was surprised because there was no man in our home.

I remained fixed to the spot as I watched him back up the stairs. He smiled and waved at me as he walked backward to the top of the stairs. Then to my further surprise, he walked to my right straight through the stairway solid wall.

Once I was able to move, I went back to the kitchen where my mother was and asked, "Mommy, who is that man on our stairs?" She asked me, "What man?" "There is no man in our house" she said, with a puzzled look on her face? Then she asked me to describe him. After describing him she gasped and told me that he was my grandfather. According to mamma, he died *shortly after I was born, and to date I have never seen a picture of him.*

I would really like to see him again in the here and now. Also, I do believe in the hereafter and know that spirits are around us through personal experiences.

A HOLIDAY NOTE

Joy, love, peace and giving is in the air as we celebrate Christmas, Hanukkah, Kwanzaa and Three Kings Day. Yet, dark clouds linger over many as we gather to celebrate. Depression sets in as thoughts of suicide fill the air. There are those that have not and would rather die than go home empty handed. They fail to see the beauty of life as they have become overcome by societal expectations. Then there are those that rob and even murder out of greed.

I say pray for others the Holiday Season, that things and gain by any means not become their focus. Pray that they understand that loving one another is what is needed and not things which will fade away.

Again pray that the innocent not become prey to the vile. Join hand in hand with others and allow peace and love to abide. For our differences gives us uniqueness and was not meant to separate.

Merry Christmas, Happy Hanukkah, Kwanzaa and Three Kings Day. For He is Lord of Lords and King of Kings.

A NOTE FOR THE HOLIDAY

Ding dong, ding dong Christmas time is near. Joy, love, peace and giving is in the air. In the spirit of Christmas we celebrate not only Christmas but Hanukkah, Kwanzaa and Three Kings Day.

This season leads us to lay aside who we are and who we think we are. It makes it ok not to know or have everything. Our status perceived or actual takes a back seat to laughter that is mingled with playfulness.

Yet, dark clouds linger over many as we celebrate. Depression sets in as thoughts of suicide fill the air. You see, there are those that have little or nothing, and would rather die than go home empty handed. They fail to see the beauty of life having become overcome by societal expectations.

Then there are those that rob and murder out of greed. They use this time of year to prey on the innocent.

Pray for others this Holiday Season, that things and gain by any means not become their focus. Pray for the innocent that they not become prey to the vile. Use this season to join hand in hand with others and celebrate our differences which gives us uniqueness.

Understand that Christmas is about the birth of Jesus and not an excuse to gain things.

Merry Christmas, Happy Hanukkah, Kwanzaa and Three Kings Day.

Reflections As Seen In Moments of Bereavements

JACOB'S LADDER

Jacob Thomas Robinson was connected to the beloved before there was a who, when or where. His name was on God's lips before taking his first breath; before his parents were chosen, before meeting his wife or having children. This humble man who had a heart filled with love; a man who believed in and served the true and living God, has climbed Jacob's Ladder to reach his father.

On the love day called Valentine's Day, Jacob T. heard his name called again and again. He wanted to stay with his beloved Izora but the call he could not resist. You see Mr. Magoo's mind was willing to hold her once more and taste of her sweetness but his body was weak. As always, he never failed to let her know that she was and will always be his lady love.

Climb Jacob, climb Jacob he heard as he began to slip from this life to eternal life. Climb Jacob for the casket cannot hold you. With the warmest smile on his face and the son of righteousness hand extended, Jacob T. Robinson climbed Jacobs Ladder and walked from Earth into his eternity.

Zora, sweet Zora was all that he said. Zora, sweet Zora, thank you my love. Thank you for all that you have done, for sharing your life with me and for caring for me. Zora, Zora, Zora, I am just a step away. I am not dead but have gained life eternal.

As the Savior promised that he did perform. He prepared a place for me and has come to receive me unto himself. Zora, Zora, Zora, I am with you always.

A LETTER OF REFLECTIONS ON JACOB ROBINSON

Jacob T. Robinson was a real man and husband to his wife Izora Robinson. He was born January 1, 1940 and departed this life on February 14, 2007. Mr. Magoo as he was fondly called by family members, was a kind, gentle and insightful man with wisdom far above his 67 years.

He loved God and family. Mr. Robinson not only made sure his wife was financially stable, but he surrounded her with a loving extended family.

You knew when you entered their home that Mr. Robinson was a force to be reckoned with. He worked hard and smart both outside and inside of their home. When his health began to fail, those performing services in his home, were yet scrutinized by his watchful eye. You could get nothing over on him.

As the illness became progressively worse, he was hospitalized several times. His wife Ms. Izora, his girls (Zoë, Jetta and Alice) would come to the hospital to visit him. We loved being around him and loved kissing him before leaving for home. When Zoë and Jetta was around, he would eat a little for them, even when he did not feel like eating. It somehow made him feel better when all his girls were around him. You see, he was a real Uncle to them and they loved him for it.

On the night before he passed, his loving wife Izora and Zorana (A/K/A Zoë) washed and dressed him. This takes love, trust and family to do and allow this to be done. Then his girls and I knelt by his bedside and prayed for him as we rubbed his head, quoted scriptures and sang songs of praise to God. We kissed him on his head before going home and told him that we loved him. Of course we kissed my sister Izora too.

When Ms. Izora called the next night to say that he had passed, Zorana and I went to their home to kiss him again and say good bye. As in life we were there for them, we wanted my sister Izora to know that she yet had us and we wanted to be there when they removed his body.

It was he who brought these two families together. When I first met him in the doctor's office where I work, he was a quiet but kind gentleman. He went home that day and told his wife about me. He said, "I hope you like her." "She is tough and a lot like you." You see, you had to pass the Ms. Izora test first to be accepted in their lives. She has a radar detector that rivals anything that mankind has made. She can size you up in three seconds. Ms. Izora doesn't take any mess off anyone.

We both are Alabama girls and outspoken. Later she told me of how I was scrutinized. I am glad that I was accepted into this loving family. Further, I am glad that my children and grandchildren are a part of this family.

Often she says, "Jacob gave me a bunch of nuts." Then she gives that hearty laugh.

I miss his genuineness and smile, but he left us a friend in his wife Izora. Now my children have a real Auntie. Jacob through God gave us someone to love and gave someone to love us back. Thank God for the gift of Jacob T. and Izora Robinson. For God makes family where he wants to.

Whenever Izora want to see Jacob T., fondly called Mr. Magoo, all she has to do is look at her son Dale.

I miss you Mr. Magoo. We miss you very much and thank God for your making us a part of your family.

LETTER TO MY FATHER

Over my many years, I have seen, heard and experienced many things. I have seen the mighty in power and even fall. I have seen morality hit rock bottom and mankind abandon their faith. I have heard your mighty words as they cut asunder the foolish words of mankind. You even blessed me with children and grandchildren.

When I did not know you as God, you kept me and even from myself. You helped me face the challenges of life and ordered my steps that my end may be better than my beginning.

Without you I would never have found my way and knew the joy of praising your name.

It was you who taught me how to work in your vineyard and to watch as well as pray. I was even given physical as well as mental strength to help me stay the course and raise my children.

When I thought that I was in charge of my destiny, you showed me that it was you who ordered my steps and you who snatched me from destruction. You were my greatest teacher, advocate and friend.

Through the sunshine and the rain your grace was sufficient. Lord of my youth and God of my old age, you have given me length of life. Not just three score and ten, but you granted me "87" years.

Even now that I have come to this juncture and to rest from the labors of my hands, well done faithful servant keep ringing in my ears.

I say thank you father for placing your mark upon my forehead and thank you for preparing a place for me. Thank you for a home that's not made by man and thank you for everlasting life. Most of all father, I thank you for the gift of Jesus which made all the difference.

To those that remain, I say that only what is done in Jesus name will stand in the end. Keep working while it is day, because soon night will come and the winds will whisper your name. He will be calling you, calling and calling you home.

*In Celebration of the Life of
Mother Mabel R. Catoe
May 12, 2007*

A LETTER OF REFLECTIONS ON MOTHER MABEL CATOE

Mother Catoe was a God fearing woman with strength of character and physical strength. I remember her introducing me to her hog. Yes I said HOG and on Michigan Avenue in Bellport, New York. She also grew collard greens that were over four feet tall. Mother Catoe was a Mabel of all trades.

I planted my first and last garden to date at her urging. I am not sure of what made me think that I could do it. Well, I did it at the expense of sore wrist, sore ankles and a sore back. She just laughed and said, "You young people aren't worth two cents." I am so glad that I was able to give her flowers while she could smell them, hold her face in my hands and tell her that I loved her and would never forget her. I'm glad that my children and one of my grandchildren would come with me to visit her and that we did not come with empty hands but brought gifts. I am glad that she knew that I was a person of integrity and believed in me.

Her allowing me to purchase her Plymouth Fury station wagon through making payments, allowed me to work and attend college.

I earned my AAS Degree in Business Administration from Suffolk County Community College and graduated with a 3.2 GPA. This was done off an 8th grade Montgomery, Alabama education and a GED. During this time I was working at The Brookhaven National Lab as an assistant to their Technicians. I shall never forget her acts of kindness.

I kept my promise mother. Your name will forever be linked with mine throughout History. Thank you for being there for me and my children.

DANIEL'S LAST CRUISE

Dear Mommy, I know that you are saddened by my passing, but don't cry for me or place blame. I know that you love and miss me dearly, but wipe your tears away. You see mommy, we all are God's children. He only loan us to each other and can reclaim us at his beckoning.

Sunday, I heard my name called and I answered. I had to go mommy and could not delay my flight. So with swiftness I spread my wings like an eagle for full flight. With eyes on God, I readied myself for this final flight. My tank was full of love when I hit the runway that I may cruise to the necessary height. With engines ready, I approached the runway; I spread my wings as my internal engine's roar blocked out calls to halt. You see, he is my father in Heaven and has the last say. I could not resist the winds of God blowing. Without fear I raised my arms and his winds picked me up. With one leap I took flight that I may soar as the eagles.

Mommy, I am not lost but found. Can't you see that death was only the doorway to eternal life? While my years were few, the joy and love that was given and received was above measure.

Always remember the feel of my ten little fingers. Close your eyes and listen for the patter of my two little feet and never forget my beautiful smile. Hold on to these memories and I will never be lost.

Don't cry for me mommy just continue to live right. One day or night you too will feel the winds blowing and your name will be called. Until then take care and be thankful for those left behind.

I love you Mommy,
Daniel
Fly high little butterfly fly high.

REST IN PEACE LITTLE ONE REST IN PEACE

TODAY IS YOUR DAY

When a young life is lost or taken we need to sit down and reflect. When multiple lives are lost or taken over a short period of time we need to dialogue with our children and others.

We need to ask ourselves, will my child be next? Ask, what lessons can be learned from such tragedies and how do I live my life from now on? Do I live to please others, worry about how other people will view me or have I finally realized that the face in the casket could be my child's or mine?

Nothing just happens! As rain comes before sunshine to bring new growth, so should this happening cause reflecting that brings enlightenment to those left behind.

If the bell had tolled for you, would you have been ready or was no thought for God or tomorrow the flavor of your day? Have you ignored the warning signs and voices of reason that attempt to influence you in your decision making process?

Young, old, saint or sinner, we all need to get ready and stay ready for the bridegroom cometh. The warning bell has rang and we that remain have been given another chance to live in a state of readiness.

Today could be your day, be careful of the choices you make.

IN A TIGHT PLACE I

There is a time and place for everything. Today I find myself in a tight place. I could complain, blame and cry poor me, but I have no complaints. Yes the cancer is obvious as is the loss of physical strength, but I have God and that makes all the difference.

When I open my mouth and speak, thank you God keep pouring out. Thank you for my childhood and adulthood. Thank you for a spouse that loved me, worked with and not against me. Thank you for children, grandchildren and their spouses. Thank you for what they are and shall become. Thank you for family, friends, experiences and that my life stands for much.

As night approaches and my work soon will be done, I thank you for finding myself in this tight place. For in tight places you carry me and you are my strength when I am weak.

Yes I walk through the VALLEY of the SHADOW of DEATH, yet I fear no evil for you are with and within me. You prepared a place for me that where you are I might dwell. When you lay me down to sleep my soul I am confident you will keep.

With tears streaming down my face, again I say, "Thank you God and thank you Jesus" for a home not made by physical hands. Thank you for new beginnings dear God; thank you for everything.

DAUGHTER TO DAUGHTER

What do I say to a daughter that I have watched day to day arrange care for her father? What words of comfort can I give her having watched the pain in her eyes at not being able to do more; heard the frustration in her voice knowing she was limited and having watched the perplexed look on her face as she knew the end was near?

Well-done faithful daughter is what comes to mind. For she gave it her all. She was on the telephone from day to day doing what a good daughter would. I say, God's blessings continue to be with you. You did the best that you could for your father, now God has taken over the rest.

I say to her that God is real and so is eternity. I remind her that God is with and within her, and will keep her in this tight place that she finds herself in.

Again I say, well done faithful daughter, well done.

In Loving Memory of Eugene J. Weston, Sr.
February 1, 2005
Name included by permission.

GOD'S MOSAIC

There is a garden that humans cannot see with the natural eye. Some say it is Eastward while others admit they don't know its' location. It contains radiant flowers that have been hand picked by God. They come from different places, are different races and ages, but all make up God's Mosaic.

Every day other gentle flowers are added to this Mosaic. Now I am left asking myself, what do I say to a mother who has outlived her child? What comfort can I give as she stands there and look down into a face that looks just like hers?

Mother to mother I say that I understand, for I have walked this road. I tell her that death has no hold on a child of God. I say that her child feared no evil for her father in Heaven's presence surrounded her child. Just like a loving father, he wraps his children in the warmth of his arms as he reclaims them. I say mother rejoice in this hard thing, because it is well with your child's soul. I say to her, that there are gates of pearls, streets of not just gold, but pure clear gold, walls of sapphire, emeralds and precious stones.

The sea of glass is real and a place has been prepared for all that believe in God.

Today we that are left behind have an opportunity to do the best we can, live the best we can and become who God has designed us to be. Tomorrow on Earth may never come our way, but his tomorrow is guaranteed.

HE WILL MAKE IT ALL RIGHT

What do you say to children who have lost their mother, siblings who have lost their sister and those who love her dearly? You say to them, hold to what you have learned from her and what you learned through God's holy words, because "He Will Make It All Right."

What do you say to a father, who year after year continues to eulogize his children and those he loves? You say to him job well done.

It was he who taught them how to live and how to serve God. He had the job of being the one who helped give them life, prayed for them on a daily basis and now is privileged by God to see them safely returned. You say to him rejoice in this hard thing, for there is no doubt that she has her crown. Not because I said so, but because the "I Am" said it.

She did not have to get ready, because she stayed in a state of readiness. She did not have to look for God, for he dwelt within her. Even when her back was against the wall, she praised God in song, dance and testimony. The same God held her tight through the sunshine and the rain.

Now through faith he has given her the victory over sin that her end is better than her beginning.

OUT OF VIEW I YET SEE YOU

Today I find myself wanting to hold you, kiss you and again say that I love you. I sit here wondering how and without my knowing you just slipped away.

Just a few days ago I found myself saying, I want my mommy, I want my mommy. Yes, as a grown woman the little girl yet lives within. Little did I know mother that so soon you would be out of my view.

With the winds of God to your back and the sun to your face you walked into God's tomorrow. You heard the call that was inaudible to my ears and quietly slipped away.

Out of view you are but through my minds eye I yet see you. Oh mother of mine, oh mother of mine I so love you.

Rest I say, rest in peace and want no more. Watch I say, for someday the winds shall whisper my name and we shall be together again. Until then I will view you through my spiritual eyes.

In Celebration of the Life of
Dorothea Moran
April 2007
Name included by permission.

I WATCHED YOU SOFTEN

While sitting here today thinking about our first meeting, I could not help but remember how angry you were. At the time I didn't know you or understand the anger. Later, I learned that it was due to your illness.

Little did you or I know back then, that we would be spending a great portion of our lives together. You as a patient and I a part of your health team.

Over time you came to see that I really cared about you and your lady love. Then I watched you soften. I watched a frown turn into a smile as you felt better and better. I watched your night turn to day and your day into night. I am so glad that I was able to watch you soften over the years.

I will miss your beautiful smile, shining eyes and kissing you on the top of the head. You sly fox, I will even miss your beautiful legs.

Now don't go flashing the heavenly host either and remember to keep down your robe of righteousness.

When the winds of God whispered your name on Saturday, June 23rd you heard and answered the call. You did not have to get ready, since you readied yourself a week ago. I saw it in your face on Friday, even as you flashed that beautiful smile.

You rallied your strength one more time and all for your beloved Lea. God allowed her to gaze into your eyes and see a restored man, not a twisted body. She was able to rub your head, kiss your lips and proclaim her love for you one more time.

As I blew you a kiss goodbye, I knew that you too knew that it would be for the last time. Eighty five years is nothing to balk at my friend, especially when you changed from a caterpillar into a beautiful butterfly.

In Celebration of the Life of
Gilbert Rodgers
June 27, 2007
Name included by permission.

VISIONS OF YOU

Thirteen years have passed since I first walked into Jackie's Lounge. As a newcomer I felt a little awkward but was soothed by the atmosphere that said welcome. While the spaces were tight it served to bring us all closer. Smiling faces in tight spaces made the atmosphere of belonging so personal.

Then Danny there was you. Your laughter was contagious as was the funny faces you made when telling jokes. We laughed to the wee hours of the morning, kidded one another, sipped drinks and every now and then you would come out and dance to the music of Felix with Linda. Once you danced even with me. Note I said once, because that took bravery. Although many came and went, most of us became family.

Every now and then you doubled my drinks and even paid the tab. You treated me like a brother keeping an eye on his sister. Oh Danny, I shall miss your smiling face, but in my mind's eye I have imbedded "Visions of You."

There were so many faces, stories and times filled with laughter. Every now and then tears also fell, but they didn't last long as you would crack a joke that made me smile.

On Monday as I kissed your head and left purple lipstick stains to match your graying hair, being Danny, you did the Danny eye roll, laughter and "oh my God," like Bill Cosby. In my heart I knew that the end was near and that soon God would whisper your name.

On Wednesday when I called to say again that you are "loved," I knew the end was even nearer. I hesitated to call on Thursday and learned that you had answered God's call to come home.

I shall miss that beautiful smile, your joking manner and gentleman behavior. I shall miss bringing you ROSES, fruit and visiting you. I shall miss you Danny my treasured friend.

Rest in peace from your labors of love; rest my friend until we meet again.

HE WAS NOT ALONE

While on Earth, we live, exist, be, do and grapple with desires, needs and wants. During this process, loved ones take flight. Those left behind reach for that they cannot see, eyes being filled with tears. Their natural senses began to fail as understanding that comes from God help them realize that dying is a part of living and life eternal is a part of God's design.

James Niebler has been blessed to come to the garden, but he was not alone. He feared no evil for God's presence surrounded him. He led him through the valley of the shadow of death that without fear James may behold his face and obtain eternal life.

Knowing this, celebrate his passing from death to life eternal. Keep the faith and walk God's way I say, for one day or night the wind too shall whisper your name. Design it will say is calling and the process of his beckoning will began again.

Keep the faith children, for there are gates of pearls, streets of not just gold, but pure clear gold. There are walls of sapphire, emeralds and precious stones too numerous to count. There is a sea of glass that only the righteous shall stand upon.

Keep the faith children, that you too may not be found wanting.

In Celebration of the Life of
James Niebler
January 20, 2008
Named included by permission.

HE NEVER LEFT ME

Now that my Earthly journey is over and life eternal is mine, I am so thankful that "He Never Left Me." In good times, bad times and even when my mother was taken, "He Never Left Me." God has never left me alone. He chose me before the foundation of this world and sealed me until the day of redemption.

All of my life, including when I did not know him as God, he guided my steps. Even when my body became wracked with pain and began to disintegrate, "He Never Left Me." It was he that brought me out of my coma, and gave me lucid moments to call on his name and see loved ones again. Jesus understood my moans and groans when my vocal cords failed and read my heart when man could not.

You see, I listened when he said, that "Love covers a multitude of faults" and "all have sinned and fallen short of the glory of God." Yes I heard him say, "Whosoever believe in him should not perish but have everlasting life." I heard him and when I called he answered and when I cried out, he said, "here I am, here I am."

Yes, Jesus loves me! He loves Jacqueline so much that when I went to the Valley of the shadows of death, I did not stay. I walked through knowing that shadows could not harm me.

Oh soul of mine, I am free from this Earthly bondage. I am safe, whole and justified. Oh to behold his face, and oh to be with my mother again.

As Jesus promised that he performed, and on September 2, 2007, he returned for me. "Free at last, free at last thank God almighty" that my soul is free from this physical body.

In Celebration of the Life of my Friend Jacqueline
September 2, 2007

ALL DONE IN MY NAME

For years you have applied your hands to the plow. You have worked in my vineyard and not just stood in pictures for show. Melvin C. Walker you have worked under the banner of my name.

Yes you preached the word in and out of season, but it was feeding the hungry, clothing the naked and visiting the sick that earned you your crown. It is your actions that will speak to your character long after hollow words spoken by man has stopped.

It was you who turned the Highway Inn into a Gospel Blessing Center and you who reached out to help others when you heard the call. I saw you climb into the back of that truck even at your age. I watched as you helped pack goods to aid the survivors of Hurricane Katrina and Rita. To the end my faithful servant you worked and it was "All Done In My Name."

As you rest from the labor of your hands, well done I say, well done.

For those that remain, I say remember that it is not what you have that will be remembered in the end, but what you have given to others in my name.

In Celebration of the Life of
Reverend Melvin C. Walker

GARFIELD'S SONG

There is a garden that no man can see with the natural eye. Some say it is Eastward while others admit, that they don't know its' location. God is the keeper of this garden and only the chosen dwell there. It contains some of the most beautiful flowers, which have been hand picked by God. Their beauty radiates love and peace that comes from God. They come from different places, are different races, ages and have different names.

A few days ago, another gentle flower was chosen to enter that garden. It seems just like yesterday that this tall gentle natured man walked in. You could not miss him even if you failed to look up. It was in the gentleness in his voice and kindness of his heart.

Little did I know that in less than four years he would be gone. Only a baby of 42, but God's child. Through his illness, he never uttered a mean word or asked me, why me? He just kept giving, being, smiling and going about his life. Never mean spirited, egotistical or prideful, this is the man known as Garfield.

While we live, exist, be, do, grapple with and become, remember the garden is just one step away. Keep trusting God who knows best. Keep the faith and continue to do your best. For as night approaches eternity slides closer and closer. Knowing this we celebrate each passing day and thank God for the likes of Garfield.

God almighty reigns forever in each life designed. Moving, choosing, keeping, enveloping and never zeroing in error.

In Celebration of a Special Man's Life

HIS BECKONING

Hand picked by God, Dorothy has entered his garden of beauty and peace. Days of pain, sorrow, grappling with needs and desires has been replaced with love, joy and peace.

Knowing this, we celebrate the passing of Dorothy Mae Robinson from death to life eternal. We are sustained by the knowledge that Death's Valley cannot hold her as she walk through its' shadow.

In the meantime, we that are left behind keep the faith and walk his way. For one day or night the wind too shall whisper our name. Design it will say is calling and the process of "HIS BECKONING" will begin again.

Dedicated To The Memory Of
Ms. Dorothy Mae Robinson
November 2003
Name included in honor of my neighbor.

I AM NOT ALONE

While on Earth, we live, exist, be, do and grapple with desires, needs and wants. During this process, loved ones take flight. Those left behind reach for that they cannot see, eyes being filled with tears. Their natural senses began to fail as understanding that comes from God help us realize that dying is a part of living and life eternal is God's design.

This is my testimony, that today; I have come to the garden, but was not alone. I fear no evil for his presence surrounds me. I have already walked through the valley of the shadow of death. I have beheld his face and obtained eternal life. I am home.

Knowing this, celebrate my passing from death to life eternal. Keep the faith and walk his way I say, for one day or night the wind too shall whisper your name. Design it will say is calling and the process of his beckoning will began again.

Keep the faith children, for there are gates of pearls, streets of not just gold, but pure clear gold. There are walls of sapphire, emeralds and precious stones too numerous to count. There is a sea of glass that only the righteous shall stand upon.

Keep the faith my children, that you too may not be found wanting.

MY JOURNEY

Life is filled with many twists and turns. My road has been long and sometimes very hard, nevertheless I have made it. I have weathered storms that those lacking faith could not and I have held on to the end. You see, I have God and that makes all the difference.

When my back was against the wall and I did not know where to turn, he was there. When my heart was heavy and I cried in the dark, he held me close. He allowed me to feel the sunshine and experience the rain. He through faith has given me the victory over sin and even death.

With the past behind me and today slowly slipping away, I know that my tomorrows with God are guaranteed. You see, I have learned that to live in this body of sin is death but to be separated from it is life eternal.

As I walk through this valley that is shadowed by death, I am not afraid. Although my body of flesh weakens, my spirit grows stronger, for my spirit feels God as he moves closer. Eternity is approaching and my journey here is over.

Listen carefully children, for one day or night you will hear the wind too whispering your name. Design it will say is calling and God is beckoning you to come to him. In the meantime, walk his way, forgive that you may be forgiven and remember that love will cover many of your faults.

In Celebration of a Special Lady's Life

SHE HEARD YOU

Ms. Lillian Small heard God's call on Friday, September 24, 2004 and she heard you too Catherine when you whispered, "Ma, it's okay to let go." Just like a mother, she needed to know that all was well and that her children would be okay. She heard you and she understood that all was well. She heard you and let go in peace.

Hand picked by God, Lillian entered his garden of beauty and peace. Her days of pain, sorrow, grappling with needs and desires have been replaced with love, joy and peace.

Knowing this, celebrate her passing from death to life eternal. Understand that Death's Valley could not hold her as she walked through its' shadow, since Jesus conquered death.

Know that she already glimpsed through God's word gates of pearls, streets of not just gold, but pure clear gold, walls of sapphire, emeralds and precious stones. She has the promise of life eternal and a place on God's Sea of clear Glass.

Armed with this knowledge, you that are left behind be sustained by God's peace. Keep the faith and walk his way I say, for one day or night the wind too shall whisper your name. Design it will say is calling and the process will begin again.

Dedicated To The Memory Of
Ms. Lillian Small
Mother of my friend Ms. Catherine B. New

ANOTHER LIFE

With an assurance I say to you, that there is life after physical death. On the day that Robert died and before the word arrived, he made his presence known. As I walked down a hall at work, two objects flew off a shelf in the near distance. Being startled, I stopped in my tracks and said jokingly, "A ghost is in that office." Others heard and saw it too.

FAMILY SOMETHING WAS AFOOT

How do you explain away a thick glass jumping off a mounted picture whose frame remains in tact? Why were two doctor figurines the only things hurled from a shelf that was filled with various figurines? I believe that it was his way of saying goodbye and in the only way that he could.

Life in a circle is all that it is. With the winds of God behind him, Robert had answered the call to come home.

May God continue to keep and guide all of us, that our end too may be better than our beginning. There is light at the end of the tunnel.

In Celebration of a Special Man's Life

VINCENZO VINCENZO

What do you say to parents, siblings and loved ones who have lost one so young? How can you hope to give them any measure of comfort? You try by saying to his mother that you know her heart is broken, since you have walked in her shoes. Tell her that God in his goodness, loan Vincent to her, both to love and be loved by him. God knew how much joy Vincenzo would bring to her heart and how much love she would give him in return. God numbered every hair on his head and bottled up every tear shed, although few. Vincent's journey is a continuing one, for before he was in your womb God knew him. Mother to mother I say, if you believe in God, you will see him again.

I say to his proud father, job well done. You loved Vincenzo well and were his rock. It was you who covered him and shared with pride his many years. Length of life is not what matters father, but the quality of life lived. It is the middle that determines the end and not the beginning. Thanks to your love and protection, Vincent has gained Eternal Life. Father, you made Vincent's life sing!

Sister, dear sister of my heart, dry your eyes and don't worry about me. I am not dead but alive through Jesus. I shall watch over you and help guide you, that your end too may be better than your beginning. As he promised that he has performed; he prepared a place for me and returned to receive me unto himself. Through his Resurrection I am alive. Now I am your angel.

Loved ones, there is a garden that humans cannot see with the natural eye. Some say it is Eastward, while others admit they don't know its' location. It contains radiant flowers that have been hand picked by God. They come from different places, are different races and ages, but all make up God's Mosaic.

You that are left behind, have an opportunity to become who God has designed you to be. Live well and come to God as children.

In Celebration of a Special Young Man's Life

A PLACE BETWEEN WORLDS

There is "A Place Between Worlds," that the natural eye cannot see. This place exists between Heaven and Earth. It is a place where spirits soar freely and you walk in both worlds.

Today I find myself in this place of peace and joy. It is a place from which, I will be watching you all.

In this place; "A Place Between Worlds," I soar with eagles and walk through walls. The impossible has become possible and I am as a child again.

Don't cry for me, for dying is a part of living that eternal life might be gained. I say that you must celebrate my new existence and joy in my resurrection.

When you feel the wind on your face and there is no wind blowing or when you smell the scent of flowers and none is in sight, know that it will be me. I am not in the grave. I am not in that physical body lying before you. Instead, I am alive in Jesus forevermore. I have the victory over sin and death.

Know that I shall be with you always. Understand that we shall be together again in God's timing.

Celebrate my life, my legacy and the space that I occupy in your hearts and you will never be without me.

In Celebration of a Special Lady's Life
Name omitted for privacy.

MY HATTIE MAE

Called by God, Hattie Mae was before the foundation of this world. She was sent to be in a place and time that would challenge the very fiber of her goodness. She has lived between Centuries and by God's grace survived some of the worst of times.

Hattie Mae, you were always my child. It was my voice you heard directing your steps even in hard times. The vessel that you emerged through, the time that you lived in and the people who touched your life was at my will. As your Earthly journey ended, it was my spirit that guided your walk through the "Valley of the Shadows of Death."

You that remain, cry not for Hattie Mae, for she is free to soar as Eagles do. It is you that need to follow my footsteps, that your end too may be better than your beginning.

Rejoice in her life and remember each curve of her smile, knowing that she is not dead but alive in me.

> *H-Home, Hattie*
> *A-at last is home.*
> *T-Total*
> *T-timing*
> *I-in*
>
> *E-every way was in force.*

———————

M-May you
A-all
E-emerge as she has.

In Celebration of a Special Lady's Life
Last name omitted for privacy.

DINA MY DINA

As my winds blow from East to West and my sun shines from hemisphere to hemisphere, I have called my Dina home.

Blessed amongst many, I have given her length of years and not just three score and ten. Beyond this, her Earthly form has been transformed to one that shall live forever.

Rejoice, I say rejoice in her life, and in her new journey. I tell you that there are gates of pearls, streets of not just gold, but pure clear gold, walls of sapphire, emeralds and precious stones. The sea of glass is real and a place has been prepared for all that believe in me.

Dina is now alive evermore! Mortal   in this realm she was, but another life now has been given her, that of immortality.

Rejoice, I say in her passing and joy in her new life. Knowing that in my world there are no limits, for through my son, I impute righteousness.

You that remain, be kind to one-another, judge not one the other, for in the end we all will face the same God.

In Celebration of a Special Lady's Life
Last name omitted for privacy.

RIDE ON JOHN RIDE ON

John was an avid bike rider, who loved to feel the winds stroke his face, wrap around his body and push at his back. His bike was his baby and riding made him feel like he could fly.

Without his knowing and without warning, early Sunday morning, John would take his last ride. He was doing what he loved to do and was so close to home, but one careless act took his life.

As the winds whipped around him the road rose up to meet him. God was at John's back, and "in a moment and the twinkle of an eye," John's bike took flight one more time and rode John into God's eternity.

Ride on John ride on the winds whispered, as his soul took flight.

Today we have the opportunity to learn from this experience. Understand that the face in the casket could be yours or mine. Know that the individual behind jail bars could be you or one of yours. The tears flowing could be from your loved-ones or for you.

People living and dying is what we all shall do, but it is what is done in the middle that will determine our end.

To those that remain behind, be watchful, be vigilant, be responsible and prayerful, for one day or night, when you too least expect, your name will be called to come home.

In Celebration of a Special Man's Life
Last name omitted for privacy.

IRMA'S WAY

Irma wore a smile that you could see from across the room. You know what I mean; a koolade smile. Sometimes it was difficult to know when she was in pain, because she disguised it so well. Irma's smile would cause you to feel better even when you did not feel good.

This woman loved God and enjoyed going to church. Sometimes I wondered how she traveled from Uniondale to Freeport or some other church function without a car. She would take a cab to church if she could not get a ride, and would figure out later how to get home.

Irma loved her children too; it didn't matter if she gave birth to them or not. She kept them well dressed, well fed and filled with her love. She was especially sensitive to the most vulnerable of her little ones. Honey, Irma kept them close to her, and yes took them to church too.

If you knew Irma, you knew that she had a great sense of style. You did not catch her at any event without looking like an African/Egyptian Queen. From her head wraps, hats and her own hair, Sister Irma was know for her style. Her dress was immaculate and her shoes and jewelry matched. She didn't wear fake fur; everything about this woman was real.

Sister Irma could eat too, but it had to be prepared right. If you don't enjoy it, then what is the sense of eating it, was one of her sayings.

She also had her fingers on the pulse of politics and would lend a helping hand when needed. Sister Irma was a kind, loving and savvy woman.

I shall miss Sister Irma's smile, I shall miss her voice, but most of all, I shall miss her honesty.

Into each life rain will fall, but after that comes the sunshine. Sister Irma has put off the old shell that was mortal and has put on the new woman of immortality. She has entered a place of no more pain, sickness or sorrow, but joy on every tomorrow. As Jesus promised, that he has performed. He prepared a place for Sister Irma, then returned to receive her unto him.

We that remain can take a lesson from her; stay ready, because time is running out. Ready or not, he will return for us someday. In the meantime, praise God in all, for when you least expect, the winds will whisper your name and it will be calling you, calling you to come home.

In Celebration of the Life of my Friend
Ms. Irma Taylor
April 16, 2008

THE CALL TO COME HOME

I thought it was the wind, but the wind wasn't inside. In a whisper, I heard my name called. For a moment I wasn't sure that I was not hearing things, but the voice again whispered Bridie, Bridie, it is time to come home. Bridie, my bride, I have come to reclaim thee.

Ninety four years I have given thee my feisty little one and with fervor, grace and determination you have lived them. You have fought a good fight in this life and have lived with dignity.

Take my hand and I'll guide you home. Take my hand and you will come to no harm. Walk with me in the light of my righteousness and I will walk you through the "Valley of the Shadows of Death." Know my child that shadows cannot harm thee.

Bridie, my Bridie welcome home.

*In Celebration of a Special Lady's Life
Last name omitted for privacy.*

THE AUDACITY OF A NATION

The year 2008 is here and the American people find themselves again at a major crossroad in History. We are on the verge of being part of a most important historical event. While we have elections all the time, this is the first time that we have the real hope of seeing a "Black/Multinational" person as President of the United States of America.

As a people, we cannot escape looking in the mirror at ourselves and our personal prejudices. We cannot skate around the issues of racism and bigotry in this country any longer. This race is not just about the race for the Presidency of the United States of America, but it is a race about race. The world is watching us and this country that consist of people of different cultures, backgrounds and nations too.

We have been brought to a place in time where we have a chance to make History. We are at the pinnacle of challenge. What we do in the November 2008 General Election will either set us back 100 years or propel us forward 100 years.

Our children are waiting and watching to see what we will do. They are listening at the words coming out of our mouths. They are hoping that for once, adults will truly take what is in their children's best interest to heart. Further, they are hoping at the end of the day that their parents surprise even themselves.

In a country of Multinational people, finally we are at the place of understanding that the culture and fabric of our country can no longer be looked at in terms of "White" dominance.

The fact that Senator Obama has been able to hold his own against the dynamic duo (Bill and Hillary Clinton) and their great army, speaks volumes to his leadership ability. I liken it to David against Goliath. I believe it clearly demonstrates his ability to remain calm and on course when and if a crises occur in this country.

The problem is not with Senator Barack Obama, but some of the old guard who have not yet gotten beyond their prejudicial beliefs and many others who are yet holding a grudge against Senator Obama, because he won the Democratic Nomination. He conducted himself beyond being a gentleman when being bombarded with negative statements made by Senator Clinton and former President Clinton.

These type are not doing this for our country or women, but for themselves. They would rather see John McCain win than to help Senator Obama, seeing that he is Black. Also it is shameful the stipulations that Senator Hillary Clinton and her supporters are trying to force on Senator Barack Obama to secure their support. It is blackmail! I am ashamed of them. This is not being done for women, but is a selfish act. I say shame on you all and ask, why would anyone want a woman as President if they have to jump through hoops and kiss their butts? These acts have set women back not forward. Now we will look very careful at ever electing a woman as President. Thanks Hillary Clinton.

We are challenged as a people to look beyond prejudice and bigotry as we enter this election season.

Our very lives, very future and that of our children and this great nation is at stake. We can no longer afford prejudicial barriers. We must help save ourselves and care not about the *face that is looking back at us, but the heart of the person who is extending their hand in true friendship and hope. We can help in the saving of ourselves if we believe in our better selves.*

I saw the picture of a smiling infant White child in the Sunday, February 10, 2008, Long Island Newsday newspaper. This child's spirit having not been tainted by others, led this child to reach a little hand up to touch the face of a person seen with gentleness of eyes. This child did not see Senator Barack Obama or a Black man, but viewed through his eyes a kindred spirit. We can take a page from this beautiful child. Together we will thrive and survive, but divided we will fail and fall. The eyes of a child are pure until shown or taught different. Let us be as children and look into the heart of these candidates when choosing the next President of this USA.

You say it is not the time to elect a Black man as President before a woman. Isn't this prejudicial thinking and aren't you implying that irrespective of a candidates abilities and qualifications, we have again determined that a Black cannot come before a White? If not now, when? If not Senator Obama, who, if it is left to the "old guard?"

Like it or not, it is inevitable that someone not termed White will lead this country as President, and not someone that will follow the lead of those of "The Old Boys Club." After all, we are more alike than others of the "old guard" would have us believe.

I lived through the era where President John F. Kennedy, Dr. Martin L. King, Jr., Malcolm X and Senator Robert Kennedy were assassinated. I lived in segregated Montgomery, Alabama and marched with Dr. King as a child. We feared Governor George Wallace, but our fears did not stop my mother, Laura Nixon from housing three Freedom marchers.

Don't fear for Senator Barack Obama because purpose and time have slapped their hands together and positioned this man in this place for this time. Further, this is a decision where his immediate and world family understands the risks. He is where God has positioned him to be. It is God who has opened this effectual door before him and has closed one behind him that he cannot go back even if he wanted to.

If the people of the great States of Alabama, Georgia, Virginia, South Carolina and Mississippi, in 2008 can vote in the affirmative to help a multinational man who is clearly "Black," win the Democratic Party's nomination to be their Presidential candidate, what is the rest of the nation's problem? If the great States of Texas, California, New York, Philadelphia, Indiana and Connecticut can provide the great amount of votes they did for Senator Barack Obama, what is the nation's problem?

If from Washington to Maryland, Vermont to Arizona this "Black" man can garnish the type of support that Senator Barack Obama has, what is the problem in this nation that is not Black or White, but Multicolored? For our children's sake it is time to deal with the skeletons in our closets and those of the past. No longer can we the people hide behind culture, religion or race. Look around and you will see that we are a combination of each other, therefore it is time to step out of the past that we may have a brighter future.

I say to you, that if you believe Senator Barack Obama is the best person for the Presidency, then vote for him. Leave his life to God as is all our lives. Further, it is what he does with the life God has given him that will count in the end.

Living on his feet is the only option that he has. Our people, African, Asian, Black and White bled, died and suffered for us through the Civil Rights Movement and slavery. Dying is easy; it is the living; what we do between birth and death that will make the difference for our children, our nation and all people.

I hope that this great nation is ready and willing to elect a person that is Multiracial. This nation should be more concerned about our economy and this ongoing war, which affects our ability to thrive and survive. We have enough problems to deal with within sub-races without creating additional race problems. Furthermore, we are concerned about our children's future, in a world of wars, rumors of unnecessary wars and multihued people. We want balance restored and a chance to mend fences with other nations. We want to co-exist with others and not dominate by fear. A rush to war comes by fools. Do you really want someone that is trigger happy and more prone to war than peace? We all better think about these candidates.

In Senator Barack Obama we see a chance for true change. After all, America is no longer and never again will be Black and White. It will forever be multihued of which Senator Barack Obama represents. Born in Hawaii to an interracial couple and having lived with and worked with people of different cultures in different nations, I believe lends a special sensitivity to world relations. Furthermore, I believe other nations will be more receptive to someone who is willing to at least meet with them. They are watching us you know.

Currently, we have a President who failed to hear the voices of the very people he was supposed to be serving. We want a President that will be more receptive to our voices and that of nations we are currently at odds with. We want someone who can understand oppression and struggle, but is not filled with anger and hatred. We need someone who will work with us, hear our voices, understand boundaries and is not seeking to conquer the world but the hearts of the people of the world.

Where the heart is, the mind follows. Point in example; when Black Americans thought Bill Clinton was like a brother, their hearts voted and stood for him.

Senator Barack Obama's foresight and willingness to be a bipartisan President, in seeking those most capable of helping him restore our nation economically, morally and to her dignity is more important than an impressive resume. Further it will give all Democratic and Republican elected officials the chance to divorce the behaviors of the "old guardsmen" and start afresh.

It is a bad assumption to believe that a person's credentials alone will make them a good leader. Point in example; George Bush. Furthermore, most of us had at least one teacher/professor or boss who was brilliant, but could not convey what he or she knew to us as students or employees. They were lousy!

Then there are very headstrong people whose attitude is one of entitlement, being always right and lacking the ability to compromise with others. This type will serve to further alienate us from other nations and further deteriorate our relationship with people in other nations, due to their inability to compromise.

This time in History will also give the American people the opportunity to prove to our elected officials that we mean business and not business as usual. It is time that they understand that they are in office to serve at the will of the people who elected them into office and not just the rich, lobbyist and special interest groups. It is time that they listen or we must rise up and vote them out of office.

The old guard is set in their ways and most believe themselves above reproach. They fail to understand that the power they have is at the discretion of the people and belong to the position and not them. This type must be shown that we will no longer tolerate their foolishness and obstinacy.

We cannot afford to hope that the old guard change. They have become rich at our expense and don't want to share the burden of restoring America. We all are in this mess and it will take all of us together to recover. What we do from now on will seal our children's future. Will it be one of failure or recovery and prosperity?

While both candidates have impressive resumes, are Senators and have professional spouses, Senator Obama is the candidate that has not been so entrenched in Washington's politics that he is no longer flexible. Also remember that people who believe that they are entitled to power are corrupted by power. "Absolute power corrupts absolutely."

We need people with ears to hear twice as much as the mouth dictates, and an individual with the ability to choose those from both sides of the isle to work with for the betterment of all life. After all, we were born human beings and not Democrats, Independents, Republicans, Liberals, Conservatives or other.

Senator Barack Obama has a heart to feel the needs of all people and the experience to redirect this country in a responsible way.

I believe, that he and his team will work to restore our nation to a place where dignity is seen along with economic empowerment and morality. He's the ONE for these times and whatever purpose he is to serve in this race, he will do by God's grace. In the end, whatever you or I think is not as important as God's will being fulfilled. Whatever that is, God's will be done.

If you believe in positive change and believe that he is "THE ONE," then vote for this visionary in the November 2008 General Presidential race. I reiterate, don't be afraid for him or of him, for we all are born for a purpose and to that end we do live.

I say, who better can represent all people, than an individual who is representative of all the people? Who will listen more readily to the wise and youth alike than someone who is both?

Neither candidate is entitled to be President. Race, age nor experience makes you entitled to a position.

Was David of the Bible more experienced than King Saul? When the prophet Samuel came to anoint the next King of Israel, all David's brothers were brought before Samuel. They were taller, older and stronger physically. Samuel said, there must be another and they began to tell of this gangly young man herding sheep. He was the one as I believe Barack Obama is today.

You see, God looks at the heart and intentions of an individual. Although Saul had enjoyed years of being King, he was not ready to relinquish the throne; not even at God's command. He sought to kill David even after the prophet Samuel had anointed David as the next King of Israel. David chose to continue to love and respect Saul, to the point that he ran as Saul sought to kill him. Why you may ask? It was because David was different and had not been overcome by power. Can you see the parallel today in the 2008 Presidential campaign?

Further, I say that you learn who people really are when they find themselves in tight places. The real man or woman comes out.

The future belongs to our children; don't sell their future for a few crumbs for yourselves. Don't sell your vote for promises that will fade away. Don't do it.

We all, especially those of us over 50 years of age, should use our remaining years, attempting to clean up the mess that many of our bad choices in people have created.

Remember this, the old guardsmen say many things in a jokingly manner to denigrate others. Then they look to those stuck shuffling their feet and dancing to the tune of yesteryear ways, to extricate them from the situation. I speak of good old Colored folk, who try to explain away boss man's words as meaning "no harm." "He just was kidding you all." My answer is, "Do you see me laughing?"

I find nothing laughable about Mike Huckabee "alleged" joke on Senator Obama. Saying, Senator Obama tripped over a chair and "someone aimed a gun at him," or Senator Hillary Clinton's reference to Robert Kennedy's assassination, as to one of the reasons she is remaining in the race for President. Yes, I said remaining. I am speaking of after Senator Barack Obama has won the Democratic nomination. Those of us who have ears to hear and eyes to see understand the strategy. That is one of the reasons many women are seen as not being trustworthy.

Those that don't have their heads buried in the sand, clearly see the racism in America as the many West Virginias clearly stated about themselves. At least they admitted that race played a role in how they voted. This is no joke and it is time that we stop laughing at things that are not funny, but degrading to people.

Our children are watching us. They are visionaries and are tired of the dancing and shuffling. They are embarrassed at the negative actions of the "old guard" and they don't want to deal with the "Crabs in a barrel syndrome." What are you teaching by your examples of hate and divisiveness? How can they sit and be seen but not heard when those who should set good examples are spewing vileness?

It is time to think and vote your conscious and stop allowing religious and political leaders to tell you how you must vote. Why? Many religious leaders' hands are deep in the pockets of the "old guard" and many politicians likewise owe religious leaders for getting their parishioners to vote for them. Where is God in this mess? I believe shaking his head in sorrow at the dysfunction of mankind.

God gave us the right of choice, I believe now is the time to use it. Whatever occurs, we all will have to live with the fall out as we have Bush.

I say to you, that in our lifetime, we may never again have this chance to truly make a difference like we have today. The people are truly being heard for once and we are speaking loudly.

This is the first time in my 57 years, that I have been this proud to be an American citizen. It is because for once in History, many of our nation's people have laid aside their personal prejudices and bigotry, to do what is best for our nation as a whole. In saying this, I understand what Mrs. Michelle Obama meant, and said regarding being proud as an adult for the first time in being an American; as does those of us who were once considered less than 1/8 human understand what she said and meant.

YOU ARE THE JURY THAT IS YET OUT, AND YOU ARE THE SCALE BALANCERS.

Special Note: I have not sought the approval of Senator Barack Obama, his affiliates or the Democratic Party in any of my writings, and I have no plans to consult with them. I have written from within. Furthermore, I will not apologize for anything that I have written unless it is proven to me that it is an error.

ABOUT THE AUTHOR

- *Born Alice Beatrice Nixon on February 23, 1951 in Montgomery, Alabama, to Laura and Samuel Nixon. She is the youngest of four children.*

- *Alice was privileged to participate in the Freedom Marches of the 60's. At approximately age 12 she participated in the Selma to Montgomery, Alabama march. Her mother housed three freedom marchers from the North at 952 Key Street in Montgomery. She will never forget Bonnie, Larry and Jerry. Bonnie and Larry were Caucasian and Jerry was Asian. She washed the blood from Jerry's shirt after he entered their home with his head bandaged. She wants the world, Asians and Blacks to know that Asians stood with Blacks and Whites in the fight for Civil Rights. She wants people to know that all races and shades of people worked together for racial equality. This is important in the healing process of the segment of Asians and Blacks that look at each other with disdain. Jerry was there. He looked at us and not down upon us. He was housed by colored folks, lived with Negroes and almost lost his life for a belief that all people deserved to be free.*

- *Her mother supported the Bus Boycott of the 1950's after the arrest of Mrs. Rosa Parks.*

- *In October 1966 she relocated to New York alone and at the age of 15.*

- *On December 28, 1967 at the age of 16 she was married to Samuel Barr Jr., whom she divorced in 1994.*

- *She is the biological mother of six children, mother of one grafted in and grandmother of five.*

- *Her faith in God helped her move from an 8th grade education to earning a 3.2 in Business Administration, a 3.0 in Administrative Justice and 4.0+ in Seminary Studies.*

- *She was Alumni speaker for the Richmond O.I.C., Richmond, Virginia in 1991 and The State University at Farmingdale, NY L.I.E.O.C. event in 1994.*

- *Alice was extended the privilege of being seated in the coveted area of the Floor of the New York State Assembly, with Assembly Members at the State of the State Address of Governor George E. Pataki in 1995.*

- *On January 21, 2002, she presented as a poet, at the Dr. Martin Luther King Celebration that was held at the African American Museum, Hempstead, New York.*

- *In 2004 she presented her piece, "Do You Remember," at the Harriet Tubman Celebration, Albany, New York.*

- *In 2007 and 2008 she was the guest speaker at one of Winthrop University Hospital's monthly Arts and Humanities Programs.*

- *She has worked such positions as Electromechanical/Electronic Assembler for such Aerospace/Electronic corporations as Vicon, Hazeltine and Grumman's Aerospace. She Interned at Brookhaven National Lab, National Synchrotron Light Source Building Upton, New York, as an Assistant to their Technicians. She also worked as Constituent Liaison and Office Manager to a New York State Assembly Member. Alice has worked various positions on the corporate ladder, including that of Secretary. She does whatever good her hands can find to do. She has advised in secret some in positions of power. All of her opportunities have been through the grace of God.*

- *Alice has guest lectured at such places as Hofstra University, Hempstead/Uniondale, New York and St. John's University in Queens, NY. She has presented as a poet in places from Southold to Albany, New York. She appears upon invitation and is also known to simply pop up. Sometimes she presents to friends who are being honored, provide poems of comfort to families at funerals and even present to the likes of Paul Rusesabagina of the movie "Hotel Rawanda" and Rubin Carter of the movie "The Hurricane."*

- *She knows what it is to be considered a have and a have not. She has been strengthened by adversity and learned how to pull herself up through God that she may achieve in-spite of hardship and instead of rolling over and dying.*

- *She believes the word of God that states, "He that finds a wife finds a good thing." Alice also believes, that the "he" should be a good thing too.*

Views of You
In Shaded Hues

A Place Between Black and White

By the Author of

The Up Side of Down

Published May 23, 2006 by AuthorHouse

Printed in the United States
206082BV00002B/136-216/P